Social Security Law in South Korea

Social Security Law in South Korea

Ji-soon Park

This book was originally published as a monograph in the International Encyclopaedia of Laws/Social Security Law.

Founding Editor: Roger Blanpain
General Editor: Frank Hendrickx
Volume Editor: Willy van Eeckhoutte

Wolters Kluwer

Published by:
Kluwer Law International B.V.
PO Box 316
2400 AH Alphen aan den Rijn
The Netherlands
E-mail: international-sales@wolterskluwer.com
Website: lrus.wolterskluwer.com

Sold and distributed by:
Wolters Kluwer Legal & Regulatory U.S.
7201 McKinney Circle
Frederick, MD 21704
United States of America
Email: customer.service@wolterskluwer.com

ISBN 978-94-035-3143-4

e-Book: ISBN 978-94-035-3144-1
web-PDF: ISBN 978-94-035-3145-8

The Author

Ji-Soon Park is a nationally recognized expert in labour law and social security law in Korea. He joined the Korea University School of Law as a professor in 2007. He earned his BA and MA from Korea University and his PhD in Law from the University of Augsburg in Germany. He has been serving as vice-chair of the Korea Society of Social Security Law since 2015, and executive director of the Korea Society of Labour Law since 2009. He is also engaged in policy advisory roles in various governmental bodies as a member of the Policy Advisory Committee at the National Human Rights Commission of Korea, the Employment Insurance Committee of the Ministry of Employment and Labour, the Advisory Committee on Human Rights Policy of the Ministry of Justice and the Public Interest Committee of Seoul National Labour Relations Commission. He is also the co-author of several books, including Labour Law (2017), Social Security Law (2017), Employee Retirement Benefits Security Act (2015).

The Author

Table of Contents

Table of Contents

List of Abbreviations

NHIS	National Health Insurance Service
NPS	National Pension Service
OECD	Organization for Economic Cooperation and Development
WHO	World Health Organization

List of Abbreviations

Preface

The history of social security law in Korea is quite short. The Korea Society of Social Security Law had not been established until 2011. The social insurance system in Korea began to take shape only after 1990, with employment insurance coming into force in 1995 and long-term care insurance in 2008. Public assistance for the poor was introduced in 2000. Still, the significance of the legal systems of social security is increasing as in other industrialized countries. Particularly in 1997, when the global financial crisis hit, Korea experienced a high unemployment rate and a recession, thus acknowledged the need for social security. The financial crisis has become an important opportunity to enforce the social security system in Korea. The laws and systems of social security continue to expand. Academic interest in social security law has also been increasing.

There is still considerable room for improvement in Korean social security law. The biggest challenge is to eliminate blind spots in the labour market. Among the whole self-employed population, which accounts for as large as 21% of all employed in the labour market, only a little proportion is covered by the national pension plan. Self-employed workers still face restrictions in joining occupational health and safety insurance as well as employment insurance. Many of the older generations who contributed to the industrialization of Korea have not joined the national pension scheme or failed to meet the required participation period as national pension system was introduced only in 1988. Often, the rights of the people living under the poverty line are not fully realized due to strict requirements for public assistance.

Korea has achieved universal health insurance, which is a rare case found in industrial countries. The actual level of protection, however, is not high. Only 64% of the total medical expenses are covered by health insurance because of financial issues of medical insurance. As a result, the burden of medical expenses is heavily laid on the population. Challenges remain in raising the level of protection of medical insurance in the future.

In Korea, social security law is consisting of numerous individual laws without being integrated into a single law. It is, therefore, a complex task to consistently explain and theorize the principles and systems of the social security law from a number of individual laws. For this reason, this monograph focuses on providing the most basic knowledge and understanding of laws and institutions that constitute the Korean social security system from the perspective of foreigners. In doing so, the monograph tries to explain each system constituting the social security law in a simple and easy way.

Preface

I am delighted to introduce the basics of the Korean social security law to other countries. I would like to express my gratitude to Kluwer Law International for giving me the opportunity. I extend my thanks to Ms Alicia Back and my assistant, Ms Doun Moon (LLM), for contributing to translating the text into English. It should also be noted that the laws mentioned in this monograph refer to the ones currently in force as of 31 December 2016.

General Introduction

§1. General Background

I. Purpose of Social Security

1. Social security is a system that pays benefits, under the responsibility of the central or local governments, to the people who need to prepare for income suspension, loss of support, and additional expenditure in case any of a variety of social accidents (disease, injury, disability, old age, death of a provider, unemployment, etc.) occurs to them. It aims to provide life security by helping them stabilize their livelihood and lead a decent life.

2. In the past, such social risks were addressed by the support of family and mutual assistance in the local community. However, the development of industrialization after the industrial revolution led to rapid social changes, such as urbanization and nuclearization of family. As a result, families were disorganized, local communities collapsed, the working class rose sharply, resulting in mass unemployment and large-scale labour accidents. The problems coming from industrialization have become social structural problems, which could no longer be solved in a traditional way.

3. These social risks have established the social security system, in which the state, instead of each individual, is responsible for ensuring basic living security of its people. Social security mainly consists of public assistance and social insurance: the former aims to help those who are already in the state of poverty and the latter aims to prepare for accidents that can happen in daily lives and put the affected individuals into poverty (e.g., disease, old age, death, disability, unemployment, etc.). In addition to social insurance, various social allowances and social welfare service systems have been created on the basis of taxation, which is not provided based on the strict investigation on the asset of the people. Their purpose is different from that of social insurance and public assistance. They are in charge of providing services to provide support for a number of difficulties in livelihood and improve the quality of life of the people, instead of preventing poverty or relieving those in need from poverty. With this in mind, it is safe to say that the purpose of social security is expanding from providing specific and practical poverty prevention and relief to ensuring the daily lives of the people facing social risks.

II. Idea of Social Security

4. Social security is a system to uphold human dignity. With the modern civil revolution, the rights to freedom and to equality emerged as core values of the Declaration of Human Rights, but behind it lies the idea of humanism, or human dignity. However, allowing human freedom and assuring equality before the law is not sufficient to maintain human dignity. To maintain one's dignity, there should be measures of any form that provide living security taken for those living in difficulty. The idea of rights to live began in the Middle Ages in the West, but initially, it played no more than an ideological role. It was in the twentieth century when the rights to live began to be prescribed in the constitutions along with rights to freedom and to equality. As such rights to live or social, constitutional rights are stipulated in the constitutions, receiving social security benefits has become the right of the people, not the favour offered by the state. And today's rights to social security have expanded from the minimum rights to lead a life to the rights assuring a life worthy of human beings where citizens can enjoy healthy and civilized lives.

5. To assure such life worthy of human beings for all its people, a country should, above all, promote and support social integration of each individual and secure momentum for social and personal development. These are the purpose of social security laws.

III. Function of Social Security

6. Social security performs a wide variety of functions, but the followings are the most representative ones: first is the function of the social safety net. Social security prevents poverty by paying appropriate levels of benefits to citizens who may fall into poverty as social risks happen to them. Second is the function of income redistribution. Social security redistributes the income that has been primarily distributed according to the purpose of social security. Under social insurance system, for instance, insurance premium cap is applied to high-income earners, and minimum benefits system is applied to low-income earners, thereby redistributing income between the two groups. The third is the function of business adjustment. For instance, during an economic boom, a part of social insurance benefits is paid as insurance premium to reduce disposable income and effective demand, ultimately preventing an excessive economic boom. On the contrary, when citizens have no more income due to social risks, social insurance benefits play a role in increasing effective demand. Fourth is the function of support for and supplement to a family function. In the past, social security was primarily the job of family members. However, with the nuclearization of family and family disorganization following the industrialization, the tasks of supporting the elderly (pension) and providing physical protection (care) are now covered by social insurance. Moreover, the role of a nation is expanding because tasks such as maternity protection and care for infants and children have been socialized as part of measures to address low birth rates.

§2. Historical Background

I. Establishment of Social Security Legislation (The 1960s)

7. Korea was liberated from Imperial Japanese colonial rule in 1945 and went through the Korean War in 1950. The country's industrialization for economic growth only began in the 1960s. During this period, a so-called growth first policy was adopted, so labour union activities demanding distribution and fundamental human rights for democracy were suppressed. In addition, the role and responsibility of the private sector were emphasized for social security, instead of that of the public sector. The social security laws made at that time were a mere gesture. A practical and detailed social security system was not implemented.

8. In Korea, the Livelihood Protection Act was first enacted in 1961 to give aid to the poor, and the Act on Social Security was enacted in 1963. Based on these laws, the enactment of the Medical Insurance Act and the Industrial Accident Compensation Insurance Act followed. However, the Livelihood Protection Act only provided partial protection of livelihood due to lack of budget, and the Medical Insurance Act had a weak base for its implementation, leading to the implementation of only four-employee health insurances (at the company level) in 1964. The Industrial Accident Compensation Insurance Act was initially applied to large places of business employing at least 500 employees in 1964 and expanded to smaller businesses employing at least 50 employees in 1969.

9. The social security laws enacted at that time were made for a political cause without consideration of social and economic conditions. As a result, the gap between laws and reality became huge.

II. Experimental Improvement (The 1970s to Mid-1980s)

10. With the end of dictatorship and the positive results of economic development, this period laid the foundation for the improvement and expansion of social security laws.

11. The Medical Insurance Act was amended in 1976, which made it compulsory for the places of business employing 500 or more employees to provide company medical insurance as of 1977. The scope expanded gradually to include the places of business employing 16 or more employees in 1982. In 1981, regional resident medical insurance was introduced as a pilot project.

12. Moreover, the National Welfare and Pension Act was enacted in 1973 to provide income security for one's later years, but its implementation was delayed for an indefinite period of time due to the oil price shock in the same year. Later in 1986, it was revised and enforced as the National Pension Act.

13. Also, more companies were required to provide industrial accident compensation insurance over time, regardless of the type of business. For instance, companies with at least thirty employees were required to provide insurance in 1972, but the number changed to at least sixteen and five employees in 1973 and 1976, respectively.

14. In 1981, the Act on Welfare of Old Persons was enacted to address the problem of the aged, and the Act on Welfare of Persons with Disabilities was also enacted later on. However, they were mostly declaratory stipulation without taking any practical measures.

III. Expansion of Social Security (Late 1980–1997)

15. After democratization movements in Korea in 1987, people became more politically aware. Also, as it hosted the Olympics in 1988, globalization was promoted. Along with these changes, Koreans grew more interested in social security. In 1988, the health insurance system started to be fully provided for residents in farming and fishing villages, and the workplaces with five or more employees were required to provide company medical insurance. In 1989, health insurance became obligatory for residents in urban communities. As a result, the national health insurance system was established, at least in the form. However, it was not sufficient to address the issue of medical security for low-income families and to solve the inequality between regional and company medial insurances.

16. During this period, industrial accident compensation insurance was applied to all workplaces except for some business, and the level of its benefits was raised. Also, the old-age allowance was created under the Act on Welfare of Old Persons, and the support for the livelihood of poor older persons began to be provided. In 1989, with the amendment of the Act on Welfare of Persons with Disabilities, assistance began to be provided to disabled persons to help them lead an independent life, and livelihood assistance allowance started to be paid. In addition, the Infant Care Act was enacted in 1991, making it compulsory for workplaces of certain sizes to establish workplace childcare facilities.

17. In 1993, the Unemployment Insurance Act was enacted for the first time and took effect in 1995. Unemployment insurance has a nature of employment insurance in that it aims to provide vocational training, prevent unemployment, expand employment opportunities and solve economic difficulties resulting from unemployment. With the implementation of this law, the so-called four major social insurance schemes were completed.

18. In 1995, the Social Security Act was enacted, providing the purpose and guidelines for the overall social security system in Korea. This Act aims to rectify unsystematic and rough nature following unplanned legislation of laws relevant to social security.

IV. Modernization of Social Security Laws (From 1997 to Present)

19. The Asian financial crisis in 1998 hit Korea, and the Korean Government experienced mass unemployment following a number of corporate restructuring. Accordingly, it became keenly aware of the need to have employment stability and establish a social safety net.

20. The scope of application of the Employment Insurance Act was expanded to all workplaces, and the amount of insurance benefits was raised. Also, separate health insurance schemes for employees, the self-employed and government employees were integrated into the National Health Insurance Act. As of 1999, a single health insurance system covering the entire population was launched. Also, the National Pension Act was amended in 1998, which was about making it mandatory for the self-employed in an urban area to hold the pension, reducing the amount of benefits to ensure the sustainability of the pension system and raising the age for commencement of receipt of a pension.

21. In 1999, the Livelihood Protection Act was completely reformed, giving birth to the Act on National Basic Living Security, which serves as the fundamental law of public assistance. Also, laws in the field of social welfare, such as the Act on Welfare of Old Persons, the Act on Welfare of Persons with Disabilities, and the Child Welfare Act, began to be amended to a great extent in 2000.

22. Even after 2000, the coverage of industrial accident compensation insurance and employment insurance (including maternity protection such as child care leave) has been further extended, and the Act on National Basic Living Security has been implemented in a full-fledged manner. In 2007, the Act on Long-Term Care Insurance for Older Persons was enacted, thereby completing the current five social insurance schemes.

V. Assessment

23. In Korea, industrialization began in the 1960s. The framework for the social security system began to be built in the 1980s, and the system became complete both in form and in quality only after 1998 after the financial crisis. However, there still are areas to be improved, especially in terms of the management of the system, such as the level of completeness of social security, the equity among members of the society, and the efficiency of the administrative system. For instance, the coverage of health insurance should be expanded, and the income replacement rate of the national pension should be maintained at a reasonable level to ensure income security for the elderly. Industrial accident compensation Insurance and employment insurance should apply to a broader group to adapt to the changes seen in today's new labour market (e.g., an increasing number of the self-employed). Nowadays, the Korean Government is seeking welfare policies to address major social changes the country faces, including low birth rates and new challenges in social security due to an ageing society (sustainability of social insurance system, in particular).

§3. Sources of Social Security Law

I. General

A. *System of Social Security Laws*

24. The Social Security Act defines the term 'social security' as well as each respective system that consists of social security. Under the Act, social insurance means 'a system that guarantees citizens' health and income by dealing with social harms that occur to citizens with insurance schemes' (Article 3(2) of the Social Security Act). Korea's social insurance system has developed in a form fairly similar to that of Germany.

25. Public assistance refers to 'a system that, for citizens who are unable to maintain a living or have difficulties in living, guarantees the minimum standard of living and supports their independence under the responsibility of the central or local governments' (Article 3(3) of the Social Security Act). The beginning of public assistance was traditionally a system that supports the poor. Unlike social insurance, public assistance is provided when an individual cannot lead a minimum standard of living on his/her own. Before qualifying as an eligible recipient of public assistance, one should first make use of his/her property, income, ability to work and support from his/her obligatory provider.

26. Social services mean 'a system that supports all citizens who need assistance from the central and local governments and the private sector by guaranteeing a decent life in the fields of welfare, health and medical service, education, employment, housing, culture, environment, and others and by providing consultation, rehabilitation, care, information, relevant social facilities, development of competence, support for social participation, and others in order to improve their quality of life' (Article 3(4) of the Social Security Act). Traditionally, social welfare is offered to those who have limited ability to perform economic, social, and daily activities on their own due to their physically or mentally special conditions (i.e., children, people with disabilities, the elderly, etc.), and its purpose is to guarantee them an equal opportunity and provide support for services needed for their living. However, the Social Security Act has expanded the concept of social welfare to include all benefits in a variety of fields provided by the nation to improve the quality of life of the citizens.

27. In addition, although not included in the definitions in the Social Security Act, the state's compensation for damages that occurred during patriotic actions, harms done by criminal acts, or other human or material damages done to individuals attributable to the entire social community also forms part of social security.

Such compensation is called 'social compensation'. Social compensation system includes the Act on the Honourable Treatment of and Support for Persons of Distinguished Service to the State and the Act on Crime Victim Protection.

B. Social Security Rights

28. The rights to social security are derived from the Constitution. Article 34(1) of the Constitution states that all citizens are entitled to a life worthy of human beings. Such life means a healthy, civilized and minimum standard of living. Moreover, Article 34(2) stipulates the nation's obligation to endeavour to promote social security and social welfare. In other words, it provides the nation's duty to provide concrete measures to assure such life worthy of human beings. However, these provisions alone do not create detailed rights to claim. When these abstract rights take concrete shape in the form of laws, the rights to claim mean the right to receive social security benefits.

29. According to Article 9 of the Social Security Act, all citizens have the right to receive social security benefits as prescribed by related statutes on social security. Such right is called social rights (Sozialleistungsanprüche). The statutes on social security refer to various laws and regulations forming social security laws. When details of social rights are determined in individual laws, people can exercise their social rights accordingly.

30. Korea's Constitutional Court made the following decision on social rights (2002HUNMA90 dated 15 May 2003):

> Article 34(1) of the Constitution assures all citizens of the right to a life worthy of human beings, and Article 34(2) clarifies the nation's duty to promote social security and social welfare. Here, 'the right to a life worthy of human beings' not only presents the ideological goal of constitutional norms for other social constitutional rights but also shows the right to demand that the State should provide minimum resources required for the citizens to ensure the minimum level of survival as human beings. The nation's duty to improve social welfare and social security is the duty imposed to come up with measures to protect its people from poverty or various disasters. In other words, it ultimately has the nature of the means to realize a life worthy of human beings. The social rights given to the people in accordance with the above provisions of the Constitution are mainly about a citizen's right to actively demand benefits from the State. Therefore, when the State enacts laws related to social rights, which distribute limited resources to its people who are in need of its protection, in order to assure its people of 'the right to a life worthy of human beings', a number of factors should be taken into consideration, such as the nation's financial soundness, social and political considerations (e.g., the overall level of social security and public sentiment), inelasticity of the system due to the long-term continuance of the system, and other characteristics of the social security system. Therefore, extensive discretion for legislation should be

granted to legislators. In conclusion, the social rights under the Constitution are developed as concrete legal rights only when details such as relevant eligibility requirements, the scope of eligible beneficiaries and the amount of benefits are stipulated in laws.

C. Legal Nature of Social Rights

31. The legal nature of social rights is different in every system, and it is not integrated. For instance, as for industrial accident compensation insurance and employment insurance, the details of insurance benefits are determined as the insurer (administrative agency) makes decisions on the benefits by due process of law, and only by then, a beneficiary obtains the right to claim the benefits from the insurer. Pension insurance has the same structure, under which a beneficiary's right to receive benefits remains abstract even if he/she has met the eligibility requirements under the laws, and the concrete right to claim is granted only when the decision (disposition) of the administrative agency is rendered. In other words, even when the requirements for the pension insurance benefits (old-age pension, disability pension, survivors' pension, etc.) are satisfied, the claim for pension payment should be first made to the competent administrative agency, and the agency should make the decision to pay the benefits before the right to claim is actually created. This is the same for long-term care insurance.

32. In contrast, health insurance, in principle, puts a beneficiary into a position to receive the benefits directly as long as he/she is eligible. Medical care benefits (treatment, nursing, etc.), which are benefits in kind, are given when healthcare institutions (hospitals, pharmacies, etc.) acknowledge that the beneficiary is an eligible insured person. They do not require any decision by the competent administrative agency for the payment of the benefits.

33. Meanwhile, the right to receive livelihood benefits under the Act on National Basic Living Security (right to public assistance) is recognized as legal rights under social security laws. The details of the right are determined by administrative dispositions of the competent local governments. The right to public assistance takes the form of 'principle of application' in that it can begin by application of a relevant person. However, when urgent protection is needed, the principle of ex officio is also acknowledged.

34. The right to social welfare services significantly involves discretionary judgment of an administrative agency, so it is considered relatively less of a right compared to social insurance or public assistance. Still, any citizen has a right to apply for the support of relevant welfare services. When such an application is made, a competent administrative agency should make a decision whether to pay the benefits or not via an administrative disposition. In that sense, the right to social welfare services can be acknowledged as a legal right.

II. Legislation

35. In general, social security laws may be deemed a public law system in which the state or a public juristic person (public organizations) is responsible for controlling the benefits that are provided for the purpose of protecting individuals from social risks. In this regard, social security laws have created their own unique field of law, which is distinguished from labour laws or tax laws.

36. Korea's Framework Act on Social Security ('the Social Security Act') defines social security 'social insurance, public assistance, and social services that assure income and services necessary to protect all citizens from social risks, such as childbirth, raising children, unemployment, old age, disability, disease, poverty and death, and to improve their quality of life' (Article 3(1)). In other words, social security is defined under positive laws as social insurance, public assistance, and social services, and the laws enacted for such social security are called social security laws.

37. Article 34 of the Constitution of the Republic of Korea provides the nation's responsibility by declaring that all citizens are entitled to a life worthy of human beings (paragraph 1) and that the nation has the duty to endeavour to promote social security and welfare (paragraph 2). In this article, social security means social insurance and public assistance in a narrow sense, and social welfare may be understood as social services. Therefore, the term 'social security' under the Social Security Act has a broad meaning, including both social security and social welfare.

38. As for the laws relevant to social security, Article 34 of the Constitution, which stipulates the right to lead a life worthy of human beings and the Social Security Act, which was enacted to guide the legislation of other social security laws and to present the ideas and fundamental directions of social security, serve as a general outline. Then, the details are added by different laws dealing with different domains of social security as follows: laws on social insurance (National Pension Act, National Health Insurance Act, Industrial Accident Compensation Insurance Act, Employment Insurance Act, and Act on Long-Term Care Insurance for Older Persons), laws on public assistance (Act on National Basic Living Security, and Medical Care Assistance Act), laws on social compensation (Act on the Honourable Treatment and Support of Persons, etc. of Distinguished Service to the State, and Act on Crime Victim Protection), and laws on social welfare services (Child Welfare Act, Act on Welfare of Old Persons, Basic Pension Act, and Act on Welfare of Persons with Disabilities, etc.).

39. Korea does not have an integrated law for social security, as is the case in Germany's Social Code (Sozialgesetzbuch, SGB). Also, it does not seem to be easy to achieve integration in the future. However, social security laws have already started to develop as a field of law, and the ideas, directions as well as specific standards for interpretation (protection of eligibility, adjustment of right to claim for damages and social rights, etc.) are being coordinated between different social security laws to conform to each other.

Part I. The Institutions

40. Each part includes a chapter about the institutions; please refer to the specific part of the chapter relevant to the topic of your interest for detailed information.

Part II. Contribution and Financing

41. Each part includes a chapter about financing; please refer to the specific part of the chapter relevant to the topic of your interest for detailed information.

Part III. Healthcare

Chapter 1. Overview

42. The Health Insurance Act was introduced in 1977. It was implemented for workplaces with 500 or more workers. Through this, the society began to take care of diseases. The treatment of a disease requires professional and costly service. Not only is a disease a cause of loss or reduction of income, but it results in the patient's loss of ability to pay the insurance premium, which is essential to care other social risks, including ageing. That is why health insurance was created; it protects the multifaceted risk profile of diseases based on social solidarity.

43. The insurance eligibility of the employee insured expanded gradually to smaller businesses. The resident of farming and fishing villages and the self-employed people in urban areas also became part of the insurance system in 1988 and 1989, respectively. With such development, health insurance has grown to be nationwide. In the meantime, the administrative system of health insurance went through fundamental changes. Health insurance had been managed in a diversified organizational system for a long time. The Employee Medical Insurance Association and the Regional Medical Insurance Association were run independently, and there was a separate public corporation for government and private school employees. After years of debate, the Regional Medical Insurance Association and the Health Insurance Management Corporation for Government and Private School Employees were merged into the National Health Insurance Management Corporation in 1998, and the National Health Insurance Management Corporation and the Employee Medical Insurance Association were merged into the National Health Insurance Service (NHIS) in 2000.

44. Today, approximately 97% of Korean citizens are governed by the National Health Insurance Act as the insured or their dependents. The rest of the citizens are protected by the Medical Care Assistance Act.

Chapter 2. Field of Application

45. Korean citizens residing in Korea shall become insured by the national health insurance except for persons who receive medical aid under the provisions of the Medical Care Assistance Act and for persons who receive medical care under the provisions of the Act on the Honourable Treatment of Persons of Distinguished Service to Independence and the Act on the Honourable Treatment and Support of Persons, etc. of Distinguished Service to the State (Article 5(1) of the National Health Insurance Act). The insured are divided into the employee insured and the self-employed insured, and the former includes public officials and private school employees (Article 6 of the Act).

46. In addition to the workers defined in the Labour Standards Act, it is mandatory for the directors and executives of corporations to become insured by the national health insurance. Since health insurance constitutes social insurance, anyone deemed unable to pay premiums cannot become the insured. For instance, part-time workers, short-time workers employed for less than sixty hours a month, and workers and employers of a workplace without a fixed location are excluded from becoming the employee insured (Article 6(2) of the Act; Article 9 of its Enforcement Decree). However, they may become the employee insured upon request therefor (Article 6(4) of the Act). Foreigners may be obliged to become or apply for becoming the employee insured or the self-employed insured (Article 109(2) of the Act; Article 76 of its Enforcement Decree).

47. Soldiers in active service, secondment personnel, and candidates for military officers are not considered as the employee insured. However, health insurance benefits are provided for their healthcare, and the costs necessary therefor are paid by the Ministry to which they belong (Article 60 of the Act).

Chapter 3. Benefits

§1. Care Provided

I. Principle of Benefits in Kind

48. The intent of the National Health Insurance Act is to provide the service necessary for the treatment of the disease and to protect the insured when the insured catch diseases (the principle of benefits in kind). This is different from another method, in which the cost of treating a disease is reimbursed (the principle of cost reimbursement). The principle of benefits in kind has two merits: first, the insured are exempted from paying the expenses first to the healthcare institution, which means medical treatment is more accessible to the insured. Second, as the insurer assumes the obligation to compensate the healthcare institution for the expenses, the insured can rid themselves of the burden of controlling the treatment of and payment to the healthcare institution. The review on the economy, efficiency and effectiveness of the treatment of and payment to the healthcare institution is conducted by the insurer. In accordance with the National Health Insurance Act, such review task is conducted by the Health Insurance Review & Assessment Service, which is an organization independent from the NHIS.

II. Co-payment System

49. The National Health Insurance Act does not cover the entire amount of medical costs of the insured. In other words, the insured need to pay part of their medical care benefits. Their share is differentiated by the type of treatment (inpatient or outpatient) and by the type of healthcare institution. As for inpatient treatments, the insured pay 20% of the total medical care benefits without exception. As for outpatient treatments, the insured pay different rates of the total medical expenses based on the type of healthcare institution where he/she received treatment (60% for tertiary hospitals, 45%–50% for general hospitals, 35%–40% for hospitals and 30% for clinics). The co-payment rates also vary when purchasing medicines at a pharmacy, depending on whether the patient has a prescription or not. He/she pays 30% of the total medicine cost in the former case and 40% in the latter case (Article 19 of its Enforcement Decree and attached Table 2).

50. The co-payment system aims to prevent deterioration of insurance finances that may be caused by excessive treatment. However, it could be the reason that the insured who lack financial resources are left untreated, exacerbating their disease. As a result, the system is untrue to the legislative purpose of the National Health Insurance Act, which is to improve citizens' health, and cannot be deemed effective in preventing deterioration of insurance finances. That is why the National Health Insurance Act stipulates a co-payment reimbursement programme. According to the programme, where the annual total amount of expenses borne by the insured and their dependents exceeds KRW 2 million to KRW 4 million based on the level of insurance premium by household (for self-employed insured) or on the level of insurance premium by an individual (for the employee insured), the excess shall be paid by the NHIS (Article 19 of its Enforcement Decree and attached Table 3).

§2. Amount of Benefit

I. Health Check-Ups

51. Health check-ups are provided in order to facilitate early detection of diseases and subsequent medical care benefits (Article 52 of the Act). Health check-ups consist of general health check-ups, cancer check-ups and infant and child health check-ups (Article 25(1) of its Enforcement Decree). General health check-ups are for the employee insured, the self-employed insured who are the heads of households, the self-employed insured who are 40 years or older and their dependents who are 40 years or older. Cancer check-ups are provided for persons who meet the check-up cycle by cancer type and age standard as set forth in the Enforcement Decree of the Cancer Control Act. Infant and child health check-ups are provided for the insured and their dependents who are 6 years or younger (Article 25(2) of the Enforcement Decree of the Act). Health check-ups are conducted at least once every two years while they are conducted once a year for the employee insured who do not have an office job. Cancer check-ups follow the provisions of the Enforcement Decree of the Cancer Control Act, and infant and child health check-ups may vary in check-up cycle and frequency in consideration of their age (Article 25(3) of its Enforcement Decree).

II. Medical Care Benefits

52. Medical care benefits cover diagnosis, medical examinations, the supply of medicines and materials for medical treatment, emergency aid, operation or other types of medical treatments, prevention, rehabilitation, hospitalization, nursing and transfers (Article 41 of the Act). Medical care benefits are provided in designated healthcare institutions, and the institutions are prohibited from denying medical care benefits without good reason. The level-one medical care benefits are reimbursed when the insured are treated in healthcare institutions other than tertiary hospitals, and the level-two medical care benefits are reimbursed when the insured are treated in tertiary hospitals. However, an emergent patient or any patient who received medical care from the Department of Family Medicine, he/she may receive level-one medical care benefits from tertiary hospitals. In general, a doctor's note stating that the patient needs to visit tertiary hospitals is required for the patient to receive level-two medical care benefits from tertiary hospitals (Article 2 of the Regulation on Medical Care Benefits).

53. Healthcare institutions, in principle, should provide medical care benefits in accordance with the standards and procedures as prescribed in the laws and regulations on the criteria for acknowledging medical care benefits. In this regard, the details are stipulated in the Regulation on Medical Care Benefits. The cost of treating diseases that are not covered by the insurance should be paid by the insured themselves ('uncovered item by the law'). In comparison, any benefits with regard to the diseases covered by the insurance that have failed to comply with the standards and procedures provided in the Regulation on Medical Care Benefits are not allowed ('discretionary uncovered item'). When the hospital receives the payment for any medical treatment that falls into the category of discretionary uncovered item, such act constitutes a 'case where a person has received medical care benefits from the insured or has made the insured to pay for the medical care benefits by deception or other unjust means' (Article 57(1) of the Act).

III. Expenses Related to Pregnancy and Childbirth

54. In addition to medical care benefits, medical expenses on pregnancy and childbirth are provided as additional benefits. The pregnant insured or the pregnant dependents may receive the medical expenses incurred in medical treatment related to pregnancy and childbirth that they received in designated healthcare institutions during their pregnancy as prenatal medical expenses. The amount payable is the amount actually borne by the pregnant insured or the pregnant dependents within the following limits: KRW 500,000 where she is pregnant with a foetus and KRW 700,000 where she is pregnant with two or more foetuses (Article 23 of its Enforcement Decree).

§3. Protected Risks: Disease and Childbirth

55. The diseases covered under the National Health Insurance Act are fundamentally based on the concept of natural science, but they are also subject to policy decisions as they present some social risks. Therefore, an illness that falls into the category of disease from a natural scientific perspective may be excluded from its category or concept based on the legislative purpose of the National Health Insurance Act. A disease under the law must meet the following three conceptual elements: first, there should be abnormal physical, psychological and/or mental conditions, and as a result, such abnormal physical, psychological and/or mental conditions go to the extent that they keep areas of the body from performing their functions as supposed to do. Therefore, simple fatigue, boredom, and a skin disease that does not interfere with one's work or daily life, for instance, do not constitute a disease. In addition, any plastic surgery not intended to treat a functional disorder is not covered under the National Health Insurance Act. Second, the need for treatment must be recognized. Treatment does not mean only a full recovery. Such need is acknowledged in any cases where any abnormal conditions cannot be eliminated or improved, or where the conditions cannot stop getting worse without medical intervention. Third, there should be curability. Even when there are abnormal health conditions, if they cannot be cured because they have become chronic or continued medical treatment is not expected to become effective, the patient with such abnormal condition will no longer be protected by health insurance but will receive long-term care by industrial accident compensation insurance or national pension.

56. The National Health Insurance Act does not directly regulate the concept and scope of diseases. It is the Regulation for Criteria for Providing Medical Care Benefits in the National Health Insurance (hereinafter the 'Regulation on Medical Care Benefits') that enumerates the items not covered by the insurance, through which the concept and scope of the diseases may be determined.

57. As pregnancy and childbirth are natural changes in body conditions, they are not diseases. Still, they affect one's economic activity similarly to diseases and require medical care.

§4. Budget Limitation

58. The health insurance is funded by, in principle, the insurance premiums paid by the insured and the employer.

59. The insurance premiums for the employee insured are comprised of the premium based on monthly remuneration and the premium based on the monthly income (Article 69 of the Act). The former refers to the amount calculated by multiplying the amount of monthly remuneration by the insurance premium rate, and the upper and lower limits thereof are put in place (Article 70 of the Act; Article 32 of its Enforcement Decree). The latter is calculated based on the amount of the extra income other than remuneration in case the amount of income of the employee insured excluding the amount of remuneration included in the calculation of the amount of monthly remuneration exceeds the amount prescribed by the Presidential Decree. It is obtained by multiplying the amount of monthly income by 50/100 (50%) of the insurance premium rate. Income from interests, income from dividends, business income, wage and salary income, and pension income are considered when calculating the premium based on the monthly income, and the insured whose annual income exceeds KRW 72 million, they become subject to the premium based on the monthly income (Article 71 of the Act). The monthly income has the upper limit of KRW 78.1 million. The premium based on a monthly remuneration of the employee insured is paid 50/50 by the employee insured and the employer. The current insurance premium rate in 2017 is 6.12% (Article 44 of its Enforcement Decree).

60. The insurance premium of the self-employed insured is paid in full by themselves. It is calculated per unit of household, and borne and paid jointly by all insured persons within the same household as the said insured. The premium of a household is obtained by multiplying the monetary value per premium point by the premium point of the household. The premium point is determined by taking into account the income, property, standard of living, and labour force participation rate of the self-employed insured (Article 72 of the Act; its Enforcement Decree attached

Table 4). The premium point is scored in a dualistic approach: for a household whose annual global income under the Income Tax Act exceeds five million won, the point is calculated by adding all the points given to their income, property and vehicle. On the other hand, for a household whose annual global income equals to or lower than five million won, the point is calculated by adding all the points given to their property, vehicle, the standard of living and labour force participation rate. Points are given in each item based on the value of the respective items, the sum of which becomes the final premium point. Then, the premium point is multiplied by the monetary value per premium point, which determines the insurance premium.

Chapter 4. Conditions

§1. Restriction of Benefits

61. Where the disease has resulted from criminal conduct through intent or gross negligence of the recipient of the insurance proceeds, or where a disease or an injury has resulted from an accident that occurred intentionally by the recipient of the insurance proceeds, the NHIS shall not provide any insurance benefits (Article 53(1) of the Act).

62. The benefits are restricted when the insured fail to perform their duty of cooperation, which is assumed to maintain the function of health insurance. For instance, in cases where a person who is supposed to receive insurance benefits has failed to follow the instructions of healthcare institutions without good reason, the NHIS shall not provide him/her with any insurance benefits. Moreover, the benefits are restricted where he/she has refused to submit the documents or other items required for the provision of the insurance benefits or evaded questions or medical check-ups (Articles 53(1), 53(2) and 53(3) of the Act).

63. When the insured fail to pay insurance premiums, the NHIS may enforce forcible collection. The NHIS may withhold insurance benefits from the self-employed insured delinquent in paying the insurance premiums for more than one month. However, this shall not apply where the total number of delinquency in paying monthly premium is below six (Article 53(3) of the Act; Article 26 of its Enforcement Decree).

§2. Adjustment of Benefits

64. For cases where the insured or their dependents receive benefits from different institutions for the same reason as they meet the requirements therefor, the National Health Insurance Act has following adjustment provisions to avoid excessive coverage: first, when a person who is eligible to receive insurance benefits has received, in accordance with the provisions of other statutes, healthcare or healthcare expenses from the central or a local government, the NHIS shall withhold the insurance benefits up to the limit of such amount (Article 53(2) of the Act). Second, when the NHIS has provided insurance benefits to the insured or their dependents because the grounds for the benefits have arisen due to the act of a third party, the NHIS shall have the right to claim compensation from the third party up to the amount of the expenses incurred for the benefits concerned (Article 58(1) of the Act). In addition, when the person who is eligible to receive insurance benefits has already received compensation for damages from the third party, the NHIS shall withhold the insurance benefits up to the amount of such compensation (Article 58(2) of the Act). Third, where he/she receives insurance benefits or compensations in accordance with other statutes due to work-related accidents, the NHIS shall not provide any insurance benefits (Article 53(1)4 of the Act).

§3. COLLECTION OF BENEFIT EXPENSES

65. When insurance benefits are provided in a wrongful manner, such benefit expenses will be collected for posterior restoration. The NHIS shall collect all or part of an amount equivalent to the insurance benefits or the insurance benefit expenses from a person who has received insurance benefits or a healthcare institution that has received insurance benefit expenses by deception or other unjust means. In case a healthcare institution has received medical care expenses from the insured or their dependents by deception or other unjust means, the NHIS will collect the money from the healthcare institution and return it to the insured or their dependents. Moreover, in case insurance benefits have been wrongfully provided on the basis of a false report or false testimony of the employer or the insured, or a false diagnosis by a healthcare institution, the NHIS may require that such person or institution pay the amount of collection jointly with the person who received the insurance benefits (Article 57 of the Act).

Chapter 5. Act on Long-Term Care Insurance for Older Persons

§1. OVERVIEW

I. Significance

66. The definition of a long-term care system varies: (i) World Health Organization (WHO) defines it as 'an integral part of health and social systems' that includes the activities undertaken for those who require care by informal and formal caregivers and volunteers, and (ii) Organization for Economic Cooperation and Development (OECD) defines it as a range of services provided over an extended period of time for senior citizens or the senior citizens who are no longer able to perform or face challenges in performing these tasks independently to help them with basic activities of daily living.

67. Korea defines its long-term care insurance a social insurance programme that provides services, such as aid in physical activities and household chores or nursing, or money paid instead of such services for an elderly person 65 years or older, or a person aged younger than 65 years but who suffers from a senile disease (e.g., Alzheimer's disease or cerebrovascular disease) by using finances of the social insurance. The purpose of this long-term care insurance system is to promote the health of elderly citizens and the stabilization of their livelihood during post-retirement life, relieve the family members from the burden of supporting them, and enhance the quality of their life for those who face challenges in performing daily activities on their own due to their age or their senile disease (Article 1 of this Act).

68. The current long-term care insurance limits its beneficiary to be an elderly person or a person with a senile disease. It is not applied comprehensively to everyone who needs long-term care, and only those granted certain grades (grades 1-5) become beneficiaries. In this sense, this programme presents limitations that only those within specific groups can benefit from it.

II. Legislation History of This Act

69. The discussion on this Act began as the Ministry of Health and Welfare formed Task Force on Policy Planning for Long-Term Care for the Elderly in 2000 and as the president officially announced the introduction of the long-term care insurance for the elderly in 2001. Later in 2004, the Executive Committee of the Public Long-Term Care Insurance System for the Elderly was established to finalize the programme, which was reviewed by the Ministry, which is in charge of senior care. The programme was submitted to the National Assembly in 2006 under the name of 'the Act on Elderly Care'. The bill was renamed as it is today, and passed in April 2007, and enforced in August 2008.

70. The initial legislation bill included the elderly as well as persons with disabilities. However, the government pointed out that the types of services required for persons with disabilities and the elderly are different, and the grading standards are different. Also, it suggested that it would address the welfare system for people with disabilities separately because such system should be part of public assistance. Consequently, the enforced Act excludes persons with disabilities from the eligible beneficiaries. However, the government established the objective of the development of long-term care insurance system in Article 5 of this Act, stating that it will endeavour to provide both elderly citizens and all citizens who suffer hardship in performing basic activities of daily living on their own, including the disabled, with long-term care benefits and services of aiding their physical activities, and will take measures to help them stabilize their living and stand on their own feet.

71. The types of long-term care system adopted by different countries may roughly be categorized: (i) by financing method, a system financed by taxation and a system financed by extra social insurance premiums; and (ii) by form, a system run as part of a nation's entire health security system and a system run independently. The long-term care insurance is often called 'the fifth social insurance program'.

§2. Protected Risks

72. The long-term care insurance for the elderly constitutes social insurance that provides services, such as aid in physical activities and household chores or nursing provided, or money paid instead of such services (the money is called 'long-term care benefits') for an elderly person 65 years or older, or a person aged younger than 65 years but who suffers from a senile disease when such person is acknowledged to have difficulties in performing daily activities on his/her own for six months or longer. In this regard, the risk protected by long-term care insurance for the elderly constitutes 'demand for long-term care', that is, one's state requiring aid in his/her physical activities and household chores or nursing services for a long period of time ('long-term care'). The demand for long-term care consists of the following conceptual elements.

73. First, the persons protected are elderly persons 65 years or older, or persons aged younger than 65 years but who suffer from senile diseases determined in statutes, such as Alzheimer's disease and cerebrovascular disease (*see* attached Table 1 of Article 2 of its Enforcement Decree). In particular, the intent of the latter part of the provision is likely that any disease listed in Table 1 would be acknowledged as a senile disease. Therefore, persons with disabilities younger than 65 years old who do not have senile diseases are not protected under the long-term care insurance. Second, one's needs for aid in physical activities and household chores or nursing should be recognized as he/she has difficulties in performing activities of daily living on his/her own for six months or longer. This concept is called the 'approval for long-term care'.

74. In order to be approved, one should first file an application to the insurer of the long-term care insurance, or the NHIS. Once the NHIS receives the application, it carries out an investigation on mental and physical conditions of the applicant, and types and details of long-term care benefits that the applicant needs. It submits the investigation results to the Long-term Care Grading Committee established under the NHIS. Where deemed necessary, the NHIS may request the competent Special Self-Governing City, Special Self-Governing Province, or Si/Gun/Gu to conduct an investigation or joint investigation (Articles 13 and 14 of this Act).

75. The approval for long-term care is an administrative action, allowing the insurer to check whether an applicant for long-term care benefits is in demand for long-term care and to grant him/her eligibility. This process is a task of the Long-term Care Grading Committee (hereinafter 'the Grading Committee'). Based on the investigation conducted by the NHIS and other documents, such as medical doctor's opinions, the Grading Committee determines the eligibility of the applicant for long-term care benefits as well as his/her grade. (Article 15 of this Act). There are five grades of long-term care, the classification of which is based on the necessity of aid or nursing. The Grading Committee's approval is effective for at least one year, and a beneficiary should file an application for the renewal of the approval if he/she wishes to continue to receive the benefits (Articles 19 and 20 of this Act). Upon the completion of examination on the approval and the grading by the Grading Committee, the NHIS should write a letter of approval for long-term care with long-term care grade, types and details of long-term care benefits, and all the other matters described therein and send it to the beneficiary (Article 17 of this Act).

§3. Beneficiaries

76. People eligible for filing an application for the approval for long-term care are the insured of long-term care insurance or their dependents, or beneficiaries of medical care assistance under Article 3(1) of the Medical Care Assistance Act (Article 12 of this Act).

77. The insured of the national health insurance automatically become the insured of the long-term care insurance for the elderly. As for foreigners, Article 93 of the National Health Insurance Act applies, which provides the regulations on foreigner's application for national health insurance (Article 7(3) of this Act). However, the NHIS may exclude foreign workers defined in the Act on the Employment, etc. of Foreign Workers and foreigners who are legally allowed to stay in Korea for technical training activities and are being trained in designated industrial establishments as set forth in the Immigration Act from persons eligible for the long-term care insurance if such foreigner files an application to be excluded (Article 7(4) of this Act).

78. Comparison of the concept of the insured as 'eligible recipient of insurance benefits' in the long-term care insurance for the elderly and the national health insurance shows the following differences in various aspects, including the details of the benefits: the latter generally covers the services provided in hospitals, clinics and pharmacies for the purposes of disease diagnosis, inpatient and outpatient treatments and rehabilitation while the former provides the persons having difficulties in carrying out basic activities of daily living on their own due to their old age or their senile diseases with services, such as assistance to their physical activities or nursing services, through intermediate care hospitals or domiciliary institutions.

79. Also, while the care services for the elderly described in the Act on Welfare of Old Persons focus more on services than the central or local governments provide in the form of public assistance for particular low-income groups, including the recipients under the national basic living security system, this Act provides services to the insured 'who are granted the approval for long-term care benefits' based on mental and physical conditions, regardless of their income level. This means that the long-term care system is a universal system.

§4. Categories and Substance of Benefits

I. Fundamental Principles of Benefits

80. With regard to the provision of long-term care benefits, this Act prescribes the principle of providing benefits according to individual beneficiary's needs, the principle of priority in domiciliary care benefits and the principle of connecting with medical services (Article 3 of this Act).

81. The first principle means that the long-term care benefits should be provided appropriately within the extent necessary for elderly citizens, taking into consideration overall factors, such as mental and physical conditions, the living environment of each elderly citizen and needs and choices of each elderly citizen and his/her family members. It is also called 'the principle of individuality'. However, considering the nature of social insurance and the actual management of the system, it is unavoidable that the social insurance benefits are generalized to some extent. That is why the system has its limits in providing the protective measures customized to fit the beneficiaries' individual situations.

82. The second principle is about prioritizing domiciliary care benefits, among other long-term care benefits, which are the benefits that an elderly citizen can receive at home while living with his/her family members. This principle seems to have taken into account that the care is most effective when provided by family members, and it may improve the role of a family. However, the recent changes in family structure have created situations that make it hard to impose the burden of the long-term care of an elderly citizen on his/her family members. That said, this principle should be applied in a flexible manner.

83. This Act stipulates that a person eligible for this insurance is an insured of the National Health Insurance Act and the criteria to determine whether he/she is in demand for long-term care are the age (65 years or older) or the occurrence of a senile disease. Therefore, it is inevitable that the benefits and protection offered under this Act and those under the National Health Insurance Act are partially overlapped. Also, it is not easy to distinguish a condition or a disease due to which a person faces difficulties in carrying out daily activities on his/her own and requires long-term care. Moreover, in some cases, a person may have the disease requiring medical action as well as the demand for long-term care. With these in mind, long-term care benefits have established the principle stating that the benefits should be provided in connection with the medical services so that the mental and physical conditions or the health of an elderly citizen do not worsen.

84. The NHIS determines the type and details of long-term care benefits to be provided to a beneficiary in a letter of approval for long-term care. In doing so, the factors considered are: the beneficiary's grade of long-term care and his/her living environment, the needs and choices of the beneficiary and his/her family members, and the current state of facilities operated by the relevant long-term care institution if such facilities are provided as benefits (Article 18 of this Act). As the plan on long-term care benefits is a very important matter to the beneficiary and his/her family members, the experts' opinions should be well reflected into the programme so that it will provide detailed and practical benefits to the beneficiaries.

85. Long-term care benefits start to be paid from the day on which a letter of approval for long-term care issued by the NHIS is delivered to the beneficiary. However, in case the beneficiary has no family member to take care of him/her, or in case there are any other reasons, the beneficiary can receive long-term care benefits even during the period between the day on which an application is filed and the day on which a letter of approval is delivered (Article 27 of this Act; Article 13 of its Enforcement Decree).

II. Categories and Substance of Benefits

86. The long-term care benefits are categorized mainly into three: domiciliary care benefits, facility benefits and special cash benefits. The classification is considered as incomplete because it is based on the type of benefits, not based on the protected risks.

A. *Domiciliary Care Benefits*

87. Domiciliary care benefits include (i) domiciliary visit care, (ii) domiciliary bathing, (iii) domiciliary nursing, (iv) day or night protection, (v) short-term protection, and (vi) other domiciliary benefits that provide or lend devices needed to support the beneficiary's daily life or physical activities (Article 23(2) of this Act). (i) Domiciliary visit care refers to long-term care benefits where a long-term care worker visits a beneficiary's home and assists his/her physical activities and household chores. (ii) Domiciliary bathing allows a long-term care worker to visit a beneficiary's home to give him/her baths. (iii) Domiciliary nursing means that a nurse working as a long-term care worker visits a beneficiary's home to provide nursing services, assist in medical treatment, give counsel on care, or treat oral hygiene in accordance with a written instruction of a medical doctor, an oriental medicine doctor, or a dentist. (iv) Day or night protection, and (v) short-term protection are the same in that a beneficiary is provided with educational or training programmes to help him/her perform physical activities or maintain and improve mental and physical functions in a long-term care institution, but the beneficiary stays in the institution for certain hours a day while under (iv) day or night protection while he/she is admitted to the institution for a certain period within the maximum period stipulated by the Ordinance of the Ministry under (v) short-term protection.

B. Facility Benefits

88. Facility benefits provide a beneficiary with educational or training programmes to help him/her perform physical activities or maintain and improve mental and physical functions after he/she is admitted to a medical welfare facility for the elderly run by a long-term care institution (Article 34 of the Act on Welfare of Old Persons) for a long term (Article 23(2) of this Act). It should be noted that these benefits do not apply to the treatment and care services due to acute diseases. In those cases, the National Health Insurance Act or the Medical Care Assistance Act is applied.

C. Special Cash Benefits

89. Special cash benefits cover family care expenses, special care expenses and nursing expenses in an intermediate care hospital (Article 23(3) of this Act). Family care expenses are the benefits paid in cash to the beneficiary when a family member or another person provides long-term care benefits equivalent to domiciliary visit care for the beneficiary who (i) lives in an area, such as an island or a remote area, in which long-term care institutions are significantly insufficient, (ii) has been recognized to have difficulty in using long-term benefits provided by long-term care institutions due to a natural disaster or any other similar cause or event, or (iii) needs to receive long-term care from his/her family members due to his/her physical or mental conditions or characters (Article 24 of this Act).

90. Special care expenses are the benefits paid in cash to a beneficiary when a beneficiary has received domiciliary care benefits or long-term care benefits equivalent to facility benefits from a care facility for the elderly or any similar institution or facility other than the designated long-term care institutions; only a part of the long-term care expenses that the beneficiary has spent is reimbursed (Article 25 of this Act).

91. Nursing expenses in an intermediate care hospital are paid to cover a part of the long-term care expenses when a beneficiary is admitted to a geriatric hospital under the Act on Welfare of Old Persons or to an intermediate care hospital defined in the Medical Service Act (Article 26 of this Act). However, special care expenses and nursing expenses in an intermediate care hospital are not being paid at this point in time because the Enforcement Decree of this Act (a Presidential Decree) and the Enforcement Regulation (the Ordinance of the Ministry) are not put in place.

92. Unlike domiciliary care benefits and facility benefits, special cash benefits are paid directly to the beneficiary in cash, which makes them weak against the protection of beneficial rights (Article 66(1) of this Act), which stipulates that a right to receive long-term care benefits shall not be transferred, seized, or offered as security to or by someone else. In other words, if special cash benefits are given to a general account in the beneficiary's name, they are mixed with other money. When the particular account is seized, the beneficiary's right to the special cash benefits and to receive the benefits is violated. That is why the law stipulates that special cash benefits should be remitted to a designated account in the beneficiary's name ('a special cash benefits account') as he/she requested (Article 27(2) of this Act), and the claim for the savings in the particular account cannot be seized (Article 66(2) of this Act).

§5. Finances

I. Insurance Premiums

93. This Act provides that long-term care insurance premiums should be collected to cover the expenses required for long-term care programme. In other words, long-term care insurance for the elderly is a type of social insurance funded by the premiums paid by the insured. The premium for the long-term care insurance is calculated by multiplying the long-term care insurance premiums rate determined through the deliberation of the Long-Term Care Committee by the amount of the national health insurance premium set in accordance with the National Health Insurance Act (Article 9 of this Act), and the NHIS should separate long-term care insurance premiums from health insurance premiums in its notice and collection, and manage the two premiums in separate accounts (Article 8 of this Act).

94. Same as the health insurance premium, the long-term care insurance premium is also determined in proportion to one's income, so it is safe to say that the premium is abated to a certain extent for low-income families. Still, low-income or vulnerable social groups may be eligible for a partial exemption of insurance premium based on certain criteria to further ease the burden. For instance, when a Grade-I or Grade-II person with disabilities registered pursuant to the Act on Welfare of Persons with Disabilities, or a person who suffers from a rare, incurable disease specified in the statutes is the insured of long-term care insurance or his/her dependent but has not been recognized as a beneficiary of the long-term care benefits, then his/her long-term care insurance premium is reduced by 30/100 (Article 10 of this Act; Article 5 of its Enforcement Decree). However, the insured who are eligible for the reduction of their insurance premium under this Act is quite limited compared to those eligible under the National Health Insurance Act (*see* Article 66(2) of the National Health Insurance Act), which calls for an adjustment.

II. Beneficiary's Pro Rata Share

95. The long-term care insurance for the elderly requires that each beneficiary bear a part of expenses incurred in relation to the insurance benefits and expenses for the areas not covered by the insurance benefits, just like the national health insurance (Article 40 of this Act). In the case of domiciliary care benefits, the beneficiary pays 15/100 of the expenses of relevant long-term care benefits and 20/100 in case of facility benefits. Nevertheless, such expenses are paid in full by the NHIS for the eligible recipients under the Act on National Basic Living Security.

96. Moreover, if a beneficiary has received long-term care benefits that are not covered (Article 14(1) of this Act) or has received long-term care benefits as he/she chose to take the benefits different from the type and details of the benefits described in his/her letter of the approval, he/she should bear, in full, such difference or the amount exceeding the monthly maximum amount of long-term care benefits (Article 40(2) of this Act). However, the beneficiary's pro rata share may be reduced depending on his/her situation. It may be abated by 50/100 (i) if he/she is a medical care beneficiary, (ii) if his/her income and property is not more than a specific amount prescribed and publicly announced by the Minister of Health and Welfare (the amount applicable to persons who reside in an island, a remote area or a rural community may be determined separately), or (iii) if he/she suffers hardships in making a living due to a natural disaster or any cause or event specified by Ordinance of the Ministry (Article 40(3) of this Act).

97. On top of that, the NHIS may abate or exempt part of the beneficiary's pro rata share of expenses or may take any other measure as a substitute for such abatement or exemption, as prescribed by Ordinance of the Ministry in case a beneficiary has been provided with long-term care equivalent to domiciliary visit care by a family member or another person, and in case the total amount of long-term care benefits so provided does not exceed an amount determined and publicly announced by the Minister of Health and Welfare (Article 41 of this Act).

Part IV. Family Allowances (Child Benefits)

§1. History and Finance

98. The Child Benefits Act was enacted on 1 September 2018, with the purpose of reducing the economic burden of fostering children, creating an environment for their sound growth, and strengthen the State's responsibilities for child care. When first enacted, the act stipulated that KRW 100,000 will be provided to those who need support among children under the age of 6. Later with the revision made on 15 January 2019, however, child benefits shall be paid to every child under the age of 7 regardless of the financial situation, in order to ensure universal financial support for any children. The State and local governments shall strive to keep child benefits at the level necessary for easing the economic burden of fostering children and creating an environment for their sound growth and shall create funds so as to bear the necessary expenses.

§2. Eligibility Requirements and Payment Periods

99. Child benefits shall be paid to be children under 7 (KRW 100,000, Article 4). A protector or an agent of a protector (hereinafter referred to as 'protector, etc.') prescribed by Ordinance of the Ministry of Health and Welfare, who intends to be paid child benefits, may apply for child benefits to the Special Self-Governing City Mayor, the Special Self-Governing Province Governor or the head of a Si/Gun/Gu (Article 6). The Special Self-Governing City Mayor, the Special Self-Governing Province Governor or the head of a Si/Gun/Gu shall determine whether to pay child benefits after verifying matters concerning the entitlement, change or loss of entitlement to child benefits through the inspection, inquiry, etc. (Article 9), and shall pay child benefits to such eligible child or his/her protector monthly from the month an application for child benefits is filed until the month immediately before the month to which his/her seventh birthday belongs (Article 10).

§3. Suspension and Restrictions

100. The Special Self-Governing City Mayor, the Special Self-Governing Province Governor or the head of a Si/Gun/Gu shall suspend the payment of child benefits from the month following the date the relevant ground occurs until the month to which belongs the date the relevant ground ceases to exist, if the period of staying abroad by an eligible child exceeds ninety days or if an eligible child is presumed to have died, as prescribed by Presidential Decree, or has gone missing or disappeared. The child benefits can also be suspended if the protector of an eligible child fails to submit or submits false documents or materials prescribed in Article 7(1), or refuses, obstructs or evades any inspection or inquiry, the Special Self-Governing City Mayor, the Special Self-Governing Province Governor or the head of a Si/Gun/Gu may suspend the payment of child benefits. In addition, the child benefits shall be suspended when an eligible child dies, loses his/her nationality or his/her refugee status granted in accordance with Refugee Act Article 2(2) is cancelled or annulled from the month following the date the relevant ground occurs.

101. The Special Self-Governing City Mayor, the Special Self-Governing Province Governor or the head of a Si/Gun/Gu shall recover the child benefits with interest in cases where (i) child benefits are received in a false or otherwise unjustified manner, (ii) child benefits are paid during the period of payment suspension, (iii) child benefits are erroneously paid due to any other cause (Article 16).

102. Note: Maternity leave is part of employment insurance in Korea's social security system. Please *see* Part VII. Unemployment for the detail of legal schemes regarding maternity leave.

Part V. Incapacity to Work

103. Incapacity to work is addressed as part of occupational health and safety insurance in Korea's legal system. Please refer to Part VI. Industrial Accidents and Occupational Diseases and Part IX. Handicapped Persons for the detail of legal schemes regarding incapacity to work.

Part VI. Industrial Accidents and Occupational Diseases

Chapter 1. General

§1. Nature of the Industrial Accident Compensation Insurance Act as a Social Insurance

104. An accident, such as an injury, disease, disability or death that happens to a worker who works in an industrial site is a social phenomenon that occurs beyond the limit of his/her individual, subjective attentiveness. It can also be seen as an event that reveals the risks inheriting in a company in today's industrial society. An employee who suffers from an industrial accident (Note: In Korea, a term 'industrial accident' is widely used, but more correct terms would be labour accident or occupational hazard in a sense that the worker suffers from an accident during labour or occupational activity. However, the term 'industrial accident' is used in this document considering the actual legal wordings.) or his/her family may plan to recover by claiming compensation for damages against the perpetrator. However, it is not easy to prove the negligence of the perpetrator under the principle of liability with fault under civil law. In this context, social legislation with regard to industrial accidents has been pursued and developed out of necessity to recognize the flaws in the compensation system under the civil law, to reflect the social characteristics of industrial accidents into the law, and to provide security in the livelihood of the victims of such accidents.

§2. The Purpose of the Act

105. The purpose of the Industrial Accident Compensation Insurance Act (hereinafter 'this Act') is to compensate the workers promptly and fairly for any occupational accident, facilitate the rehabilitation of workers suffering from occupational accidents and their return to society, and carry out projects aiming at preventing accidents and promoting workers welfare by providing a variety of insurance benefits (Article 1 of this Act). This Act has the nature of social security in that (i) it imposes the liability without fault for occupational accidents upon employers, (ii) it standardizes the compensation and specifies its amount, (iii) in principle, the costs related to the compensation are covered in full by employers, and (iv) employers are covered by an insurance system controlled by the government as policyholders.

Chapter 2. Field of Application

§1. Territorial Field of Application

106. This Act applies to all the businesses or places of business that employ workers (hereinafter 'Business'). However, this Act is not applied to certain businesses in consideration of their risk rate, size, place and other factors (Article 6 of this Act). Above all, this Act does not apply to public officers, teachers and staff of private schools, and sailors, who will be covered by other laws in case of accidents. Moreover, it does not apply to workers who are hired for constructions performed by non-professional builders, the total construction cost of which is below KRW 20 million; for construction of buildings whose total floor area is 100 square meters or below; for remodelling construction of buildings whose total floor area is 200 square meters or below; or for housework services.

§2. Personal Field of Application

107. The owners of the Business subject to this Act are the insured of the industrial accident compensation insurance ('the Insurance'), and the workers hired by the Business are the beneficiaries of insurance benefits. The definition of workers in this Act is the same as that in the Labour Standards Act (Article 5(2) of this Act).

108. If the insured (business owners) applies for an insurance policy for persons dispatched to work in a Business run by the insured in a foreign country ('persons dispatched overseas'), and if such application is approved, Korea's Insurance applies to such persons dispatched overseas (Article 122 of this Act). In addition, on-the-job trainees, who are not workers but receive on-the-job training in a Business as part of vocational training, are regarded as workers and, therefore, covered by the Insurance. Moreover, foreign workers are protected by this Act as long as they work in a Business subject to this Act. It does not matter whether such foreign workers have a valid visa to stay and work in Korea.

109. Furthermore, this Act applies to some freelancers, who are not acknowledged as workers under the Labour Standards Act but who are deemed equivalent to workers in their economic relationship with business owners and therefore need to be protected. These freelancers are referred to as 'persons in special types of employment'. This Act provides that the freelancers, such as insurance solicitors, owner-drivers of concrete mixer trucks, learning-aid tutors, golf caddies, door-to-door couriers, express delivery riders, loan solicitors, credit card solicitors, and persons engaging in a designated driving service, are covered by the Insurance (Article 125 of this Act; Article 125 of its Enforcement Decree).

110. Meanwhile, in principle, a business owner cannot be the beneficiary of insurance benefits. However, the owner of small- or medium-sized enterprises may become the beneficiary after obtaining the approval of Korea Workers' Compensation & Welfare Service ('the Workers' Service') under certain requirements (Article 124 of this Act). In this case, such owner is regarded as a worker for the application of this Act.

Chapter 3. Concept of 'Industrial Accident'

§1. Accident

111. The requirement to receive insurance benefits under this Act is to have an occupational accident. An occupational accident means any injury, disease, disability or death of a worker caused by an 'occupational' reason (Article 5(1) of this Act). It is an important matter to determine whether an accident is caused by an 'occupational' reason or not when it comes to making decisions on the existence of liability for compensation and the details of the benefits between the labour and the management. A precedent interpreted an occupational accident as 'an accident that resulted from duties or ordinary activities that accompany the duties as a worker under his/her employment contract with his/her business owner, and under control and supervision of the business owner, in the process of performing such duties or activities' (Supreme Court Decision No. 97Nu13009 dated 14 November 1997), establishing two requisites for an occupational accident, i.e., whether the accident was related while performing one's duties and whether the accident resulted from such duties. This Act currently in force take the perspectives of various precedents into consideration and provides the standards for recognition of occupational accidents in this Act (Article 37) and its Enforcement Decree (Articles 27 through 36) in detail. These provisions mainly classify occupational accidents into accidents on duty and occupational diseases.

Chapter 4. Concept of 'Occupational Disease'

§1. Types of Occupational Disease

112. Types of occupational diseases include any disease caused by handling or being exposed to any physical agent, chemical substance, dust, pathogen, work putting a burden on a worker's body, or any other agent causing trouble to his/her health while performing his/her duties; any disease caused by an occupational injury; and any other disease caused related to his/her duties.

113. Occupational diseases are mainly classified into an accident-related disease, which has an accident on duty as a medium between work and disease, and a work-related disease (vocational disease), which does not. As for the former, the accident results in the disease, so the factors such as time and place of the occurrence of the disease are clearly known. On the contrary, the latter is affected by harmful elements and risk factors inherent in the work over a long period of time, so raise an issue of proving the causal relationship between the work and the disease.

114. Therefore, the Enforcement Decree of the Labour Standards Act and the Enforcement Decree of this Act stipulate the scope of occupational diseases to reduce the burden of proof on workers suffering from occupational accidents and facilitate the protection of the rights for vocational diseases (Article 44 and its attached Table 5 of the Enforcement Decree of the Labour Standards Act; Article 34 and its attached Table 3 of the Enforcement Decree of this Act). Accordingly, occupational diseases are classified broadly into diseases illustrated in detail in Table 3 of the Enforcement Decree of this Act and other diseases clearly resulting from one's duties ('unillustrated diseases').

115. The illustrated diseases specify in detail the diseases that are confirmed, under social norms, to be closely related to workers' duties and match the diseases with certain duties. Therefore, the causal relationship can be assumed as long as a worker suffering from an occupational accident proves that he/she engages in certain duties and has developed a disease corresponding to the duties. However, this precedent takes a stance that a disease can be recognized as an occupational disease even if it does not meet the criteria set forth in Table 3 (Supreme Court Decision No. 2012Du24214 dated 12 June 2014).

116. Unlike the illustrated diseases, the proximate causal relationship between his/her duties and the accident is not assumed for the unillustrated diseases, so the burden of proof is on the worker suffering from the occupational accident (Supreme Court Decision No. 97Nu7011 dated 5 September 1997; Supreme Court Decision No. 96Nu14883 dated 28 February 1997). Nevertheless, it is not easy for a worker, who lacks medical and professional knowledge, to prove the causal relationship between his/her duties and disease. Also, changes in industrial structure, rapid technological innovation and rationalization have increased the possibility of the outbreak of new vocational diseases. For these reasons, the burden of proof has been eased over time (Supreme Court Decision No. 2006Du4912 dated 12 April 2007).

§2. Karoshi

117. Strictly speaking, Karoshi is not a legal concept, but it is a collective term referring to the cases in which a worker's death resulting from the fatigue, which has been built over time from physical overwork or psychological stress related to his/her duties. Therefore, the legal issue over karoshi is whether a death due to overwork on duty can be recognized as occupational accidents subject to this Act. The main factor of karoshi is accumulated physical fatigue and psychological stress coming from the qualitative change of labour, and reinforced production management and labour density. Therefore, karoshi is different from a sudden death, which is an accident due to an external cause, or from death from a vocational disease, which has been found relevant to harmful factors of certain duties.

118. Still, accident-related diseases or vocational diseases may overlap with karoshi because they can emerge by combining with overwork. In particular, one of the important causes of karoshi is physical features of individual workers or any disease they may have already had. Moreover, karoshi is particular in that the cause of overwork is not clear, whether it comes from professional or personal lives. With this in mind, it is a huge challenge to determine which criteria to apply in order to recognize karoshi as an occupational accident. According to the Supreme Court, the proximate causal relationship between worker's duties and the accident should be determined based on health and physical conditions of the concerned worker, not of an average worker, and clear proof from medical and natural scientific perspectives is not required to prove such relationship. The proximate causal relationship is deemed proven when such relationship is concluded, by interference, to exist after taking various factors into consideration (Supreme Court Decision No. 2011Du3944 dated 9 June 2011).

Chapter 5. Commuting Accidents

§1. Overview

119. Korea's Constitutional Court (Decision No. 2014Hunma254 dated 29 September 2016) judged that it is against the principle of equity to recognize only the accidents that occurred while using the means of transportation provided by the employer because it discriminates against other workers who got into accidents while using other means of transportation. Accordingly, the law was revised so that various types of accidents occurring during a commute are recognized as a category of 'Commuting Accidents' along with two other categories of 'Industrial Accidents' and 'Occupational Disease.'

§2. Requirements

120. The term 'commuting' means a movement between a residence and a place of employment or from one place of employment to another place of employment in relation to employment (Article 5(8)). 'Accidents' include: (i) any accident that occurs while he/she commutes to or from work using transportation means provided by his/her business owner or another similar means under the control and management of his/her business owner; and (ii) any accident that occurs while he/she commutes to or from work using other common route and method. However, for the latter, any accident occurred during a deviation or a suspension of the regular commute shall not be deemed an accident on commuting except when the deviation or suspension is an action necessary for daily life prescribed by Presidential Decree (e.g., purchasing daily necessities, job training, voting, medical appointments, child care, nursing for family members, etc.). Also, the provision is not applicable to a type of work that does not have a regular route and method as prescribed by Presidential Decree.

Chapter 6. Types of Insurance Benefits

§1. Medical Care

121. Medical care benefits (for treatment and medicine) are provided to a worker who suffers from an injury or a disease caused by a reason related to his/her duties. (However, the benefits are not paid if such injury or disease can be fully recovered through treatment within three days. Article 40(1) and 40(3) of this Act). Medical care benefits should cover the medical expenses in full, and the workers should be treated in care facilities established by the Workers' Service (hospitals specialized in industrial accidents) or general medical institutions designated by the Workers' Service. However, the medical expenses may be paid in lieu of the medical care in extenuating circumstances (Article 40(2) of this Act). If a person who has received medical care benefits gets to suffer a recurrence of the occupational injury or disease, which was previously the object of the medical care, after the injury or disease was cured, or if a medical opinion is presented that his/her injury or disease has worsened and, therefore, needs active treatment to cure it, he/she may receive 'recurrent medical care' (Article 51 of this Act).

122. Nursing benefits are paid to a person, among those who have received medical care benefits, who is in need for constant or frequent nursing care from a medical point of view after his/her full recovery, and who is currently receiving nursing care (Article 61 of this Act).

§2. Temporary Lay-Off Benefits & Injury-Disease Compensation Annuities

123. Temporary lay-off benefits are offered for a period during which a worker was unable to work for receiving medical care (excluding the cases where workers were unable to work for up to three days), and the amount of benefits per day is an amount equivalent to 70/100 of his/her average wage (Article 52 of this Act). In case a worker receiving medical care is employed for a certain period of time or on a short-term basis during the period of such care, he/she is paid an amount equivalent to 90/100 of the amount calculated by subtracting the wages for the days or hours employed from his/her average wage corresponding to the number of such days or hours employed (Article 53 of this Act).

124. If a worker receiving medical care benefits remains not fully recovered from the injury or disease even two years after the day on which he/she started to receive the care if the level of his/her disability caused by such injury or disease corresponds to disability grades prescribed in a Presidential Decree (Attached Table 8 of its Enforcement Decree), and if he/she fails to find employment due such care, he/she will be paid injury-disease compensation annuities instead of temporary lay-off benefits (Article 66 of this Act).

§3. Disability Benefits

125. If a worker suffers from physical or mental disability after fully recovering from any injury or disease caused by an occupational reason, he/she is paid disability benefits. Disability benefits are paid in the form of disability pension or lump-sum disability compensation according to disability grades. The criteria for disability grades are prescribed in a Presidential Decree (Article 57 of this Act). Since the amount of disability benefits varies depending on disability grades, the decision on a worker's disability grade is practically the most important matter. Article 53(1) and its attached Table 6 of the Enforcement Decree of this Act stipulate that there are 14 grades according to the degree of loss of labour ability. Such decision on disability grades is made when a worker's symptoms remain unchanged following the termination of the care (Article 46(10) of its Enforcement Regulation). If a worker's disability grade, which has already been determined, has a potential to change as his/her condition has improved or worsened, his/her disability grade may be re-determined upon the request of such eligible recipient or ex officio (Article 59 of this Act). When the decision on disability grades has made without complying to laws and regulations, it may become the subject of administrative litigation (Supreme Court Decision No. 2004Du12957 dated 22 February 2007).

§4. Survivors' Benefits & Funeral Expenses

126. Survivors' benefits are paid to the family of the deceased if a worker dies of an occupational reason, and they are paid in the form of survivors' pension or lump-sum survivors' compensation. However, the latter is paid only if there is no person eligible for survivors' pension. If an eligible recipient of survivors' pension wishes, an amount equivalent to 50/100 of the lump-sum survivors' compensation is paid in a lump sum, and the survivors' pension is paid in an amount reduced by 50/100 (Article 62 of this Act).

127. Among the survivors whose livelihood had been supported by such worker at the time of the worker's death (excluding those who were not Korean nationals and were living abroad at the time of such death), the spouse (including a person in a de facto marital relationship), parents or grandparents aged 60 years or older, children or grandchildren under 19 years of age, siblings under 19 years of age or aged 60 years or older, and any person who is either a child, parent or sibling who does not fall under any of above classifications, and who has at least a second-degree disability, are eligible to receive survivors' pension. The order of priority to receive such pension is as follows: spouse, children, parents, grandchildren, grandparents, and siblings (Article 63 of this Act).

128. When a worker dies of an occupational reason, funeral expenses are paid. The amount of the expenses is an amount equivalent to 120 days of his/her average wage, and it is given to the person who arranged the funeral services (Article 71 of this Act).

§5. Vocational Rehabilitation Benefits

129. Vocational rehabilitation benefits are offered to promote vocational rehabilitation of persons with disabilities who suffer from occupational accidents and their return to work. The types of the benefits include: (i) vocational training costs and vocational training allowances for persons who require vocational training to be employed ('trainees') among persons who have received disability benefits or pneumoconiosis pension, or who are clearly expected to receive disability benefits as prescribed by Presidential Decree ('recipients of disability benefits'); and (ii) return-to-work subsidies, training costs to adapt oneself to work, and rehabilitation exercise costs that are paid respectively if a business owner retains employment or carries out a training programme to help adapt to work or a rehabilitation exercise programme for the recipients of disability benefits who return to the Business for which they worked when the occupational accident occurred (Article 72 of this Act).

130. Vocational training for the trainees is provided by a vocational training institution contracted with the Workers' Service (the insurer), and the costs needed for the training are paid to the institution (Article 73 of this Act). Vocational training allowances are given to the trainees receiving the vocational training for a period of their unemployment, and the amount paid per day is equivalent to the minimum wage (Article 74 of this Act).

131. Return-to-work subsidies, training costs to adapt oneself to work, and rehabilitation exercise costs are paid respectively to business owners that retain employment of the recipients of disability benefits or that provide work adaptation training programmes or rehabilitation exercise programmes for such recipients. The amount of return-to-work subsidies is the amount that business owners have paid to the recipients of disability benefits within limits officially announced by the Minister of Employment and Labour in consideration of wage levels and conditions in the labour market, and their payment period is limited to twelve months. The amount of work adaptation training costs and rehabilitation exercise costs is the actual costs needed within limits officially announced by the Minister of Employment and Labour in consideration of the costs required for such training and exercise programmes, and their payment period is limited to three months (Article 75 of this Act).

Chapter 7. Restrictions on Insurance Benefits

132. If a worker under medical care violates instructions on his/her care without any valid reason, thereby worsening the injury, disease or disability condition or preventing full recovery, or if an eligible recipient of disability pension worsens his/her disability condition on purpose, such as through self-harm, prior to the re-determination of his/her disability grade, he/she may not receive all or part of the insurance benefits (Article 83(1) of this Act).

133. This Act stipulates that any intentional action, self-harm or a criminal act of a worker or any injury, disease, disability or death of a worker caused by such an act is not deemed an occupational accident. (However, if such injury, disease, disability or death is caused by any act committed in the state where his/her normal cognitive function was remarkably declined, it is considered an exception and therefore deemed an occupational accident; Article 37(2) of this Act).

Chapter 8. Relations to Other Compensation and Indemnity under Other Laws

134. If eligible recipients have received or can receive insurance benefits under this Act, the insured is exempted from any further liability for compensation for the same cause under the Labour Standards Act. If eligible recipients receive insurance benefits under this Act for the same cause, the insured is exempted from any further liability for compensation under the Civil Act or other laws and regulations within the limit of the amount of such benefits. Also, if eligible recipients receive other money or valuables, which correspond to insurance benefits under this Act, for the same cause under the Civil Act or other laws and regulations, the Workers' Service does not pay insurance benefits under this Act within the limit of the amount calculated by converting the money or valuables so received according to the method determined by Presidential Decree (Article 80 of this Act).

135. In case the Workers' Service has paid insurance benefits to a worker for an accident caused by an act of a third person, it exercises the right to claim compensation for damages against the third person within limits the amount of such benefits on behalf of the person who has received such benefits. If the third person has compensated damages to the worker suffering from an occupational accident, the Workers' Service does not pay insurance benefits under this Act within the limits of the amount of the damages converted by the method prescribed by Presidential Decree (Article 87 this Act).

Chapter 9. Insurance Finance

136. In principle, the costs needed for the industrial accident compensation insurance business are borne, in full, by business owners (the insured). To this, the government bears costs to a certain extent. The details with regard to insurance premium and other funds collected to cover the insurance business are stipulated in the Act on the Collection, etc. of Premiums for Employment Insurance and Industrial Accident Compensation Insurance (Article 4 of this Act).

137. Insurance premium is collected from business owners to cover the costs for the insurance business, and such premium is calculated by multiplying the total amount of remunerations of the Business run by such business owners by the industrial accident compensation insurance premium rate applied to the same kind of business (Article 13(1) and 13(5) of the Act on the Collection, etc. of Premiums for Employment Insurance and Industrial Accident Compensation Insurance).

138. However, with regard to the persons in special types of employment who are subject to special cases, their status is freelancer, so the person and his/her business owner pay 50/100 each for the insurance premium.

139. The insurance premium rate is determined on 30 June every year, based on the proportion of the total amount of industrial accident compensation insurance benefits to the total benefits for the past three years. Also, the following elements are factored in to determine the rate: the amount required to pay such insurance benefits, including pensions under this Act, the costs for accident prevention, and the costs to promote the welfare of workers suffering from occupational accidents. Then, the rates are determined by the type of business and prescribed by the Ordinance of the Ministry of Employment and Labour.

140. This Act has put in place a system that either increases or reduces the insurance premium rate according to the frequency of industrial accidents at the business for the purpose of encouraging business owners to make an effort to prevent industrial accidents. Under this system, if the proportion of the amount of industrial accident compensation insurance benefits to the amount of the insurance premium for the past three years corresponds to the proportion as prescribed by Presidential Decree, the rate is raised or reduced as set forth in Presidential Decree up to 50/100 of the premium rate currently applied to the Business. Then, the new rate can be used as the insurance premium rate for the Business for the following insurance year.

Part VII. Unemployment

Chapter 1. Provision of Work

§1. Assistance for Job Creation & Assistance for Employment Adjustment

141. The Minister of Employment and Labour may provide assistance to a business owner who has expanded employment opportunities by improving the working environment or changing work patterns (Article 20 of this Act).

142. In addition, the Minister may provide necessary assistance to a business owner who has faced an inevitable situation for employment adjustment due to downsizing, closing or conversion of his/her business following the changes in the economy or industrial structure and has taken measures for his/her employees' job security, such as the temporary shutdown of the business, temporary lay-off of the workers, vocational skills training for a career change, or manpower redistribution. Moreover, if workers' wages are decreased due to the abovementioned measures for employment stability, such as temporary shutdown or temporary lay-off, to a level prescribed by the Presidential Decree, then necessary assistance may be provided to the said workers (Article 21(1) of this Act). The types of assistance for employment adjustment include subsidies for employee retention and re-employment assistance for a person whose employment is to be severed.

I. Subsidies for Employee Retention

143. The Minister of Employment and Labour grants subsidies to a business owner who has faced an unavoidable situation for employment adjustment, has taken certain measures to retain his/her employees who are the insured and has not severed them during the period where the employment retainment measures are taken and one month thereafter (Article 19(1) of its Enforcement Decree). A business owner who wishes to receive such subsidies is required to establish and implement plans for retaining employees in compliance with certain requirements (Article 20(1) of its Enforcement Decree).

II. Re-Employment Assistance for Person Whose Employment Is to Be Severed

144. When a business owner who finds it inevitable to carry out employment adjustment independently or jointly establishes the facilities or contracts out to an external organization equipped with the facilities needed to provide services to support rapid re-employment of 'insured workers who have been employed by the relevant business but whose employment will be severed due to employment adjustment, retirement or expiration of the term of employment contract,' or 'workers who had been insured and employed by the relevant business but whose employment was severed due to employment adjustment, retirement or expiration of the term of employment contract', he/she may receive part of the incurred expenses (Article 22 of its Enforcement Decree).

§2. Assistance for Employment Promotion

145. The Minister of Employment and Labour may provide assistance to a business owner who has relocated his/her business to, or founded or expanded his/her business in a region where employment situation is rapidly deteriorating due to a significant lack of employment opportunity or changes in industrial structure, thereby contributing to preventing unemployment and promoting re-employment in the region, or a business owner who has taken measures to increase employment opportunities in the region (Article 22 of this Act).

146. Moreover, the Minister may provide the necessary support to a business owner who hires seniors or those who find it particularly difficult to get a job or takes measures necessary for their employment stability, or an employee who has benefited from the employment stability measures taken by such business owner (Article 23 of this Act). The assistance for employment promotion programmes offer the subsidies for the employment stability of the elderly, the vulnerable social group, the female workers and those on child care leave, and they include various types such as subsidies for extension of employment of seniors, subsidies for employment of seniors aged 60 years or older, subsidies for employment promotion, subsidies for wage peak system, and subsidies for employment stability during the period of childbirth and child care (*see* Articles 25 through 29 of its Enforcement Decree).

§3. Assistance for Vocational Skills Development Training

147. Vocational skills development programmes allow employees to constantly improve their job performance at work, making their workplace both a place to work and learn. The purpose of these programmes is to improve labour productivity and raise wage levels of the employees, and they are mainly divided into the assistance to business owners and the assistance to employees. The Minister of Employment and Labour may provide a business owner who runs vocational skills training programmes to help the insured workers develop and improve their vocational skills with the expenses needed for such training (Article 27 of this Act). Meanwhile, the Minister may provide funds to the insured workers who participate in the training or make an effort to develop and improve their vocational skills to cover necessary expenses, and may run such training programmes to promote the employment of insured workers, if deemed necessary. Low-income insured workers may have loans granted to cover their living expenses when they participate in training for vocational skills development (Article 29 of this Act).

Chapter 2. Unemployment Benefit

§1. Objective and Nature

148. This Act aims to contribute to economic and social development by implementing employment insurance. The purpose of the insurance is to prevent unemployment, promote employment, develop and improve vocational skills of workers, reinforce the government's role in vocational guidance and job placement services, and provide unemployment benefits to ensure the stable livelihood of unemployed workers and to encourage them to look for a job (Article 1 of this Act). Preventive and active in nature, the current employment insurance system connects and implements employment security programmes and vocational skills development programmes on top of unemployment insurance in the conventional sense.

149. This Act was enacted in 1993 and came into effect in 1995.

§2. Insurance Relation

150. The owner and employees of the business to which this Act applies naturally to become the insured of the employment insurance. If an owner of a business to which this Act does not apply wishes to have him/her and his/her employees join the employment insurance programme, the owner is required to receive the consent of a majority of the employees and obtain the approval of Korea Workers' Compensation & Welfare Service pursuant to the provision of Article 8 of this Act (Article 5(1) and 5(2) of the Act on the Collection, etc. of Premiums for Employment Insurance and Industrial Accident Compensation Insurance). Moreover, an employer with no employees, an employer with no more than fifty employees, or a self-employed person meeting the requirements prescribed by the Presidential Decree may join the insurance programme after obtaining the approval of Korea Workers' Compensation & Welfare Service (Article 49-2 of the Act on the Collection, etc. of Premiums for Employment Insurance and Industrial Accident Compensation Insurance).

151. The insured of the employment insurance are the employees and the self-employed who have subscribed to the insurance. This Act does not apply to a person who was employed or self-employed after the age of 65, a person whose monthly contractual working hours are lower than sixty hours (including a person whose weekly contractual working hours are lower than fifteen hours), a public official defined in the State Public Officials Act or the Local Public Officials Act, a person subject to the Act on Pension for Private School Teachers and Staff, or a foreign worker who falls into a certain category as set forth by law (Article 10 of this Act, Article 3 of its Enforcement Decree).

152. The insurance programme is governed by the Minister of Employment and Labour (Article 3 of this Act).

§3. Field of Application

153. An unemployed person in the sense of the employment insurance is defined as a person in the state of being unemployed despite one's ability and willingness to work (*see* Article 2(3) of this Act). The unemployment benefits are provided to ensure the stable livelihood of unemployed people and to facilitate their job-seeking activities. Such benefits are paid to the beneficiaries only when they engage in job-seeking activities with intent and ability to perform work and when they have paid their premiums for a certain period of time. The main types of unemployment benefits are job seeker's allowance and employment promotion allowance.

154. Following the amendment of this Act in July 2011, a self-employed person is now able to receive unemployment benefits (Articles 69-2 through 69-9 of this Act).

§4. Categories and Substance of Programmes

155. The programmes under this Act are mainly categorized into the following: employment security and vocational skills development programmes, unemployment benefits, child care leave benefits, and others.

156. The purpose of the first category is to prevent unemployment, promote employment, increase employment opportunities, provide opportunities and assistance to develop and improve vocational skills, ensure employment security and help employers find stable workforce (Article 19(1) of this Act). In addition, unemployment benefits are provided to help unemployed persons stabilize their livelihood, encourage them to find a new job as soon as possible and help them develop their vocational skills (Article 37 of this Act). Moreover, child care leave benefits and benefits for reduced working hours during child care are given to encourage both male and female workers to jointly participate in the care of their child and to find a balance between career and parenting without losing their jobs because of child care (Articles 70 and 73-2 of this Act). Furthermore, maternity leave benefits are offered as part of maternity protection to ensure the employment stability of female workers (Article 75 of this Act).

§5. Amount of the Benefit

I. Job Seeker's Allowance

A. *Eligibility Requirements*

157. Job seeker's allowance is the most fundamental and important benefits among the unemployment benefits and is provided for stability of an insured person's livelihood while he/she is unemployed. It is paid when the insured person who was severed from his/her job had been insured for 180 days or more in total during

18 months prior to his/her unemployment, and when he/she is in the state of unemployment despite his/her ability and intent to work and despite active efforts to find a new job. However, when the person left his job voluntarily or was dismissed for a serious cause attributable to him/her, he/she is not eligible for the allowance (Articles 40 and 58 of this Act).

158. Anyone who intends to receive job seeker's allowance should report, without delay, his/her unemployment status to an employment security office upon the severance from employment (Article 42 of this Act), and be approved by the head of the employment security office that he/she is an eligible beneficiary (Article 43 of this Act). To be recognized of unemployment, eligible beneficiaries need to be present on a day designated by the head of the employment security office between the first and fourth week counting from the date of reporting their unemployment and report that they have made an effort to find a job. Then, the head of the employment security office recognizes each day between the next day following the most recent unemployment recognition date and the date of unemployment recognition. Job seeker's allowance is provided only for the days of unemployment recognized by the head of the employment security office among the period of a beneficiary's unemployment (Article 44 of this Act).

B. Substance and Period of Benefits

159. The amount of job seeker's allowance is calculated based on the per diem amount equivalent to 50/100 of 'basic daily wage', which is daily wage to be used as the basis for computation of the allowance (Articles 45 and 46 of this Act). Unless otherwise stipulated in law, the allowance is paid for the certain number of days, as specified in the law, up to twelve months following the date of one's severance from employment to which the current eligibility for the said allowance relates (Article 48 of this Act).

160. It can be extended up to two years in case the vocational training directed by the head of the employment security office is still in progress (Article 51 of this Act, Article 72 of its Enforcement Decree). Moreover, the number of days for the allowance can be extended in view of situations of individual workers (who find it particularly difficult to get a job, and who live in financial hardships) and situations in the general labour market (e.g., the rapid increase of unemployment) (Articles 52 and 53 of this Act).

C. Restrictions on Eligibility

161. In the case where the head of an employment security office recognizes that an insured person falls into any of the following categories, he/she is deemed ineligible for job seeker's allowance (Article 58 of this Act):

(a) an insured worker who was dismissed for a serious cause attributable to him/her, who was sentenced to imprisonment without labour or greater punishment because of his/her violation of the Criminal Act or any duty-related laws, who caused serious damage to the business or its property, or was absent at work without notice for a long time in breach of the employment contract or employment rules without due cause (Article 58(1) of this Act); or

(b) an insured worker who left work voluntarily to take up a new job or to start one's own business, who resigned following the business owner's suggestion instead of being dismissed for a serious cause attributable to him/her as discussed above, or who resigned for any reason not deemed due cause pursuant to the Ordinance of the Ministry of Employment and Labour (Article 58(2) of this Act).

D. Restrictions on Benefits Payment

162.

(a) The payment of job seeker's allowance is suspended if a beneficiary refuses to accept a job offered by the head of an employment security office, refuses to participate in vocational skills training as directed by the head of an employment security office, or refuses, without any reasonable cause, to follow the vocational guidance provided by the head of an employment security office to facilitate re-employment in accordance with the criteria determined by the Minister of Employment and Labour (Article 60(1) of this Act).

(b) If anyone has obtained or has attempted to obtain unemployment benefits by fraud or other unlawful means, the payment of the allowance is suspended from the day on which he/she received or was supposed to receive such allowance (Article 61(1) of this Act).

II. Employment Promotion Allowance

163. Employment promotion allowance is classified into early re-employment allowance, vocational skills development allowance, long-distance job search allowance and relocation allowance (Article 37(2) of this Act).

164. Early re-employment allowance is offered to an eligible recipient who secures a stable job or starts one's own for-profit business in case where the eligible recipient was re-employed before the half of the allowance payment days has passed as of the day preceding the date of re-employment after the waiting period, and then the recipient has been employed or has engaged in his/her own business for at least twelve consecutive months. The amount of the allowance is calculated in proportion to the remaining number of days for the payment of job seeker's allowance, based on legal standards (Article 64 of this Act, Article 84 of its Enforcement Decree). Vocational skills development allowance is provided while an eligible recipient participates in vocational skills development training programmes required by the head of an employment security office (Article 65 of this Act). Long-distance job search allowance is paid, when deemed necessary by the head of an employment security office, to an eligible recipient who engages in job search over a wide area as guided by the employment security office (Article 66 of this Act). Relocation allowance is offered, when deemed necessary by the head of an employment security office, to an eligible recipient who moves his/her residence to get a job or to take part in vocational skills training directed by the head of the employment security office (Article 67 of this Act).

A. Child Care Leave Benefits and Others

165. Since its introduction in November 2001, the provisions related to child care leave benefits have undergone multiple amendments. Today, the benefits are provided to male and female employees who are granted a parental leave of more than thirty days (excluding the period overlapping with the maternity leave period pursuant to Article 74 of the Labour Standards Act) to raise a child (including an adopted child) aged 8 or under or who is in the second grade or under at an elementary school, and the amount of the benefits is 40/100 of the monthly ordinary wages (upper limit: KRW 1 million per month, lower limit: KRW 0.5 million per month) (Article 70 of this Act; Article 95 of its Enforcement Decree). Moreover, an insured person who reduced his/her working hours during child care for more than thirty days in accordance with the Act on Equal Employment Opportunity and Work-Family Balance Assistance (excluding the period overlapping with the maternity leave period pursuant to Article 74 of the Labour Standards Act) can be provided with benefits for reduced working hours during child care (Article 73-2 of this Act). Both benefits are provided when the days qualifying for the insurance as of the beginning date of the child care leave is 180 days or more, and when an insured worker's spouse, who is also an insured worker, has not been granted child care leave of 30 days or more for the same child, has not reduced his/her working hours during child care for 30 days or more (Articles 70 and 73-2 of this Act).

166. A pregnant worker should be granted a maternity leave of 90 days (120 days if she is pregnant with at least two children at a time) before and after childbirth. Also, when a pregnant worker asks for the leave due to her experience of miscarriage or stillbirth, such leave should be granted as prescribed by the Presidential Decree (Article 74 of the Labour Standards Act). In case a female worker with the days qualifying for the insurance prior to the last day of the maternity leave is 180 days or more received a maternity leave before and after childbirth or miscarriage or stillbirth leave, the Minister of Employment and Labour grants her maternity leave benefits or miscarriage or stillbirth leave benefits corresponding to the ordinary wages under the Labour Standards Act for the period of such leave (Article 18 of the Act on Equal Employment Opportunity and Work-Family Balance Assistance, Article 75 of the Employment Insurance Act).

§6. Conditions

167. The Minister should not provide a person who has obtained or has attempted to obtain assistance for employment security and vocational skills development programmes by fraud or other unlawful means with the granted subsidies or the remainder of the subsidies that have already been provided to him/her. In addition, the Minister should restrict the payment of the subsidies within the period as prescribed by the Presidential Decree up to one year, and should order him/her to return the amount of subsidies that have been provided to him/her by fraud or other unlawful means (Article 35(1) of this Act).

§7. Insurance Finance

168. The insurance premiums are collected from the insured, i.e., business owners and their employees, to cover the expenses of the employment insurance programme. An employee and his/her employer pay each half of the premiums for unemployment benefits, and the employer pays the premiums in full for employment stability and vocational skills development programmes. However, a person who is employed or self-employed after the age of 65 is exempted from paying the insurance premiums for unemployment benefits (Article 13 of the Act on the Collection, etc. of Premiums for Employment Insurance and Industrial Accident Compensation Insurance).

169. The Minister of Employment and Labour establishes the Employment Insurance Fund to finance insurance programmes, and the Fund is raised by insurance premiums, payments collected under this Act, reserve funds and the Fund's earnings and other sources of income (Article 78 of this Act).

170. The government covers part of the annual expenses for the insurance programmes (Article 5(1) of this Act).

Part VIII. Pensions

Chapter 1. General

§1. Significance

171. Incidents in our daily life, such as old age, disability or the death of the bread earner, lead to loss of or decline in income or the state of loss of support for a long time, threatening the livelihood of an elderly person, a person with disabilities or the family of the deceased. Pension system is an income security programme to prepare for such events. Its purpose is to provide benefits replacing the income to maintain one's life stable when a risk of a long-term income loss occurs, such as old age, disability or the death of the provider. The system consists mainly of the private pension system and the public pension system. The former includes a personal pension, which an individual enters into voluntarily with a private insurance company, and a retirement pension, which a company joins for its employees under the Act on the Guarantee of Workers' Retirement Benefits. The latter includes occupational pensions for those working in special occupations, including public officials, soldiers, private school employees and special post office employees, and the national pension plan for the rest of the general public. The two pension systems are managed separately, and each pension system has slightly different functions, conditions for benefits and substances. The most significant features of the public pension system are that the subscription is mandatory for all members of the society and that the level of benefits should secure a basic income level even in one's later years.

172. Korea's leading public pension system is the national pension plan. It is social insurance enforced in accordance with the National Pension Act ('this Act'). In principle, the national pension plan covers Korean nationals aged between 18 and under 60, excluding those insured by occupational pensions. The insured is divided into the workplace-based insured person and individually insured person. The contributions for the former are paid by the insured person and his/her employer while those for the latter are paid by the insured person only. Pension benefits are categorized by insurance risk: old-age benefits, disability benefits, survivor's benefits, and others. The pension system has implemented so-called sliding scheme of pension (or adjustment scheme), which factors in elements in proportion to one's income and reflects the changes in annual consumer price index into the level of pension benefits, to ensure basic income level in one's old age.

§2. BENEFICIARIES

173. A Korean national, who resides in the territory of Korea and who is aged between 18 and under 60, is insured under the national pension plan (Article 6 of this Act). However, a person protected by another law from the same social risks protected under this Act is excluded from the coverage of the national pension plan (the proviso of Article 8(1) of this Act). In other words, this Act does not apply to a person insured under the Public Officials Pension Act, the Military Pension Act or the Act on Pension for Private School Teachers and Staff. Nevertheless, in case a person granted the right to receive benefits, such as retirement pension, under this Act ('person eligible for retirement pension') files an application for the aggregation of the entitlement periods of two pensions in accordance with Article 8 of the Act on Aggregation of National Pension and Occupational Pensions, the person becomes eligible to be insured under this Act. Furthermore, in accordance with Article 61(1) of this Act and Article 2 of the supplementary provision of the wholly amended National Pension Act, an employee under 60 years old who has been engaged in a special occupational category and has acquired entitlement to the old-age pension pursuant, and a person who has acquired entitlement to the early old-age pension referred to in Article 61(2) of this Act are excluded from the coverage of the national pension plan. However, a person for whom the payment of the early old-age pension is suspended pursuant to Article 66(1) of this Act becomes eligible to join the pension plan (Article 18 of its Enforcement Decree).

174. Any Korean national eligible for the national pension plan is mandatorily insured either as a workplace-based insured person or an individually insured person. If he/she falls into neither, he/she can join as a voluntarily insured person or a voluntarily and continuously insured person (Article 7 of this Act). A workplace-based insured person means a person who subscribes to the national pension plan as an employer or an employee (*see* Article 8(1)1 and 8(1)2 of this Act) in a workplace covered by the National Pension Service (NPS) (*see* the main text of Article 8(1) of this Act). An employer means the business owner of a workplace to which a relevant employee belongs (Article 3(1)2 of this Act), and an employee means a person (including directors or other executive officers of corporations) who offers his/her labour and services in a workplace, irrespective of the type of occupation, and receives wages in return for his/her labour and services (Article 3(1)1 of this Act). However, a person who is employed on a daily basis or for a specified period of less than one month, a person who is employed in the workplace of which location is not fixed, a director of a corporation without a fixed remuneration, or a part-time worker whose contractual working hours are less than sixty hours in a month is not deemed an employee, and his/her subscription to the plan as workplace-based insured persons is not mandatory. If a person who falls into one of the abovementioned categories of short-time workers has continued to work for more than three months to make a living, such as a part-time lecturer under Article 7(3) of the Enforcement Decree of the Higher Education Act, and if he/she wishes to be deemed an employee with the consent of the employer, he/she may join the national pension plan (*see* Article 2 of the Enforcement Decree of this Act).

175. Among the eligible nationals, a person who is not a workplace-based insured person automatically becomes an individually insured person. However, a non-income earner whose spouse falls under any of the categories prescribed in Article 9(1) of this Act, a beneficiary of a retirement pension, a person aged between 18 and under 27 and who has no income because he/she is a student or in military service, a recipient of assistance under the Act on National Basic Living Security, or a person whose whereabouts are unknown for at least one year are excluded from becoming an individually insured person (Article 9 of this Act). Even if one is not deemed a workplace-based insured person nor an individually insured person, he/she can become voluntarily insured if he/she files an application before turning 60 years old (Article 10 of this Act). Furthermore, if a person currently or formerly insured by the national pension plan who has reached age 60 but is yet eligible to receive a pension as he/she has been enrolled in the plan for not long enough, or if a person who has worked in a special occupational category and acquired entitlement to a special old-age pension but wishes to prolong his/her term to receive a higher amount of the pension, then he/she may become voluntarily and continuously insured by filing an application for membership until he/she reaches age 65 (Article 13 of this Act).

176. The Statistics on National Pension announced by the NPS state that the number of subscribers to the national pension plan as of the end of September 2019 is 22,139,572, 63.7% of which (14,103,712) are workplace-based insured persons, 32.5% (7,214,206) are individually insured persons, 1.5% (331,638) are voluntarily insured persons, and 2.2% (490,016) are voluntarily and continuously insured persons.

§3. Protected Risks

177. The reasons for which the benefits are provided under this Act or the risks protected under this Act are old age, disability and death. Among the risks, the insurance risk of old age means an insured person has reached a certain age where he/she is no longer able to carry out normal income-earning activities due to physical or social reasons. It is different from other contingent accidents, such as disability or death, in that it is predictable and a number of people in the same generation reach the age at the same time. The thing is that when the job of preparing for old age is left to individuals, each individual makes different levels of efforts, including savings, and one's own effort may not be sufficient. Consequently, countries have come up with a variety of designs of a public system to ensure income in old age. The most basic methods are insurance and social allowances funded by tax.

178. Unlike old age, disability and deaths are unpredictable insurance risks whose time of occurrence cannot be specified. In a sense, the need to secure income in these cases may be higher than the case of old age. To this end, disability pension is paid based on the degree of disability for as long as the disability persists for a person who suffers from a physical or mental disability despite having fully recovered from a disease (referring to cases where the date of the first medical examination on the relevant disease occurs within the insurance coverage period, including cases where an insured person was unaware of the outbreak of a disease at the time he/she became insured) or injury that occurred during the insurance coverage period (Article 67(1) of this Act). Moreover, when a person died, and if he/she was a beneficiary of an old-age pension, an insured person who paid for the pension for ten years or more, an insured person, or a beneficiary of a disability pension who had at least a second-degree disability, survivor's pension is paid to his/her surviving family. However, if the person who died of a disease or injury had held the pension plan for less than one year, survivor's pension is paid only where such death is caused by a disease or injury which arose during the insurance coverage period (Article 72(1) of this Act). Therefore, the time of occurrence of a disease or injury is an important yardstick for judgment in this case.

§4. Categories of Benefits & Eligibility Requirements

179. The benefits under this Act are categorized mainly of old-age pension, disability pension, survivor's pension and lump-sum refund to cover the risks of old age, disability and death, respectively (Article 49 of this Act). The lump-sum refund is paid when an insurance risk occurs, or a reason for the loss of eligibility arises to an insured person who has failed to meet the requirements to receive benefits.

Chapter 2. Old-Age Pension

§1. Beneficiaries

180. Old-age pension may be divided into full old-age pension, reduced old-age pension, active old-age pension, and early old-age pension based on coverage period, the age for commencement of receipt of pension and a beneficiary's involvement in income-earning activities. One should meet both requirements in order to receive old-age pension: one has to reach a certain age, and that one has contributed to the pension plan for a certain period of time.

181. Full old-age pension starts to be paid once an insured person whose insurance coverage period is 20 years or more reaches the age for commencement of receipt of a pension (refer to the following). Its amount is the sum of basic pension amount and dependant's pension amount (Articles 61(1) and 63(1)1 of this Act).

182. Reduced old-age pension starts to be paid once an insured person whose insurance coverage period is at least ten years but less than twenty years reaches the age for commencement of receipt of a pension (Article 63(1)2 of this Act). Its amount equals to 50/100 of basic pension amount plus dependant's pension amount. For each year exceeding the insurance coverage of ten years, an amount equivalent to 5/100 of the basic pension amount is added, which leads to 100% of basic pension amount once the coverage period reaches twenty years.

183. When an insured person whose insurance coverage period is ten years or longer is engaged in activities that generate income over a certain level during the period where he/she is at least 60 years old but less than 65 years old, he/she is eligible to receive an active old-age pension (Article 63(2) of this Act). The problem with this pension type is that a beneficiary with income in addition to pension benefits may receive excessive benefits if he/she engages in income-earning activities after he/she reaches the age for commencement of receipt of a pension. To this end, the pension benefits paid to beneficiaries generating income should be controlled to curb unnecessary spending of pension finance while the amounts of pension benefits between beneficiaries who engage in and who do not engage in income-generating activities should be adjusted to ensure income redistribution and to promote justice.

§2. Pension Calculation

I. Principles

184. The amount of pension is calculated by adding a basic pension amount with dependant's pension amount, the purpose of which is to meet the family demand. Basic pension amount is the sum of an 'equal part' based on the average income of all insured persons regardless of an individual's income level and an 'income proportionate part' based on one's average income during his/her coverage period. This is to redistribute the income by reducing the income gap of low-income and high-income groups. For a low-income group, the pension amount is calculated on the basis of an average monthly income (Value A), which is an average monthly income of all insured persons for the three years prior to receiving pension benefits, and for a high-income group, the pension amount is calculated based on standard monthly income (Value B), which is an average monthly income of the insured person during his/her insurance coverage period. Then, the respective amount is multiplied by the insurance coverage period, resulting in the basic pension amount for each individual insured person. For reference, Value A from March 2016 to February 2017 is KRW 2,105,482.

185. Dependant's pension is provided to protect dependents whose living was supported by a beneficiary of pension at the time when the beneficiary acquires or after he/she has acquired the entitlement to benefits, or to protect the family of the deceased who is not a beneficiary of survivor's pension when the insured person dies. The amount of dependant's pension is prescribed at a fixed amount for the spouse, child and parent of the deceased. KRW 150,000 per year is given to the spouse, KRW 100,000 per year to the child under 18 or with at least a second-degree disability (including any child born to or adopted by the spouse before marriage), and KRW 100,000 per year to the parent aged 61 years or older, or with at least a second-degree disability (including the spouse of the father or mother, and parents of the spouse) (Article 52 of this Act). The dependant's pension amount is adjusted according to the fluctuation rate of nationwide consumer price index as is the case for the basic pension amount (*see* Article 52(2) of this Act).

II. Old-Age Pension and Early Old-Age Pension

186. The amount of active old-age pension is calculated only based on basic pension amount, without adding dependant's pension amount. In other words, an insured person whose insurance coverage period is twenty years or more is given an amount equivalent to 50/100 of basic pension amount, and an amount equivalent to 10/100 of the basic pension amount is added each year. An insured person whose insurance coverage period is less than twenty years is given an amount equivalent to 50/100 of basic pension amount. This means that when he/she reaches 60 years old, he/she is paid 50/100 of the basic pension amount as an active old-age pension, and 10/100 of 50/100 of the basic amount is added every year. Meanwhile, there has been criticism that the current reduced old-age pension is based on age, which has a negative effect on giving beneficiaries an incentive to work, and that the criteria of age irrelevant to income fails to accomplish the initial goal of the system. Hence, the preparations for an amendment are underway to change the criteria for the reduction from age to income level, so that a lower reduction rate may be applied to a beneficiary with lower income, and a higher reduction rate may be applied to a beneficiary with higher income.

187. Early old-age pension is provided for current or former insured persons whose coverage period is ten years or longer. When he/she is 55 years or older and not engaged in income-earning activities, and if he/she wishes to receive this type of pension even before turning 60, he/she may do so during the remaining lifetime. When an insured person whose coverage period is twenty years or more decides to receive the pension at the age of 55, the amount of early old-age pension is 70/100 of basic pension amount plus dependant's pension amount. When one's coverage period is less than twenty years, he/she may receive 50/100 of basic pension amount plus dependant's pension amount. For instance, when he/she decides to begin his pension receipt at the age of 55, 6/100 of basic pension amount is added every year until he/she reaches 60 years of age.

III. Divided Pension

188. One of the controversies over the public pension system was the status of an ex-spouse under this Act because this Act did not have any provisions on the legal status of the former spouse regarding the right to claim for pension benefits that his/her spouse, who is the insured person, acquired during the marriage. The dominant view was that the pension benefits (severance pay) that the insured spouse has already acquired and possessed might be subject to the claim for division of property under the Civil Act. However, the amendment of this Act in 1998 introduced a system acknowledging the ex-spouse's right to claim for division of old-age pension. A considerable number of countries recognize the future division of pensions to the parts that a spouse contributed during the marriage.

189. When a person who has been married for at least five years (limited to the marriage period during which one's spouse is under insurance coverage) divorced his/her spouse, when his/her former spouse is a beneficiary of an old-age pension, and when the person reaches age 60, he/she may receive divided pension during his/her lifetime, which is a portion of his/her former spouse's old-age pension. The amount of divided pension is the amount obtained by equally dividing the amount of pension corresponding to the period of marriage out of the former spouse's amount of old-age pension. However, the amount of dependant's pension is excluded therefrom. The right to claim for the divided pension lapses three years after the claim for the division is established (Article 64 of this Act).

190. The claim for divided pension follows the occurrence of the former spouse's entitlement of old-age pension, but it does not require a court judgment or does not lapse after the death of the former spouse. The problem can be the fact that the divided pension amount is not calculated based on the income at the time of the divorce. Still, the division is done in a manner that ensures objectivity and rationality as it is difficult to accurately compute the present value of pension benefits equivalent to the period to which a spouse has contributed during the marriage.

191. When a beneficiary of divided pension becomes entitled to two or more divided pensions, he/she shall be given the combined total of the two or more divided pensions.

192. This Act amended on 29 December 2016 (enforced on 30 December 2016) introduces new Article 64-2, which provides that any decision made with regard to the division of pensions pursuant to the right to claim for division of property under the Civil Act should be respected. Its intent is to allow the blameful spouse, who is liable for the divorce, to be paid less pension benefits. When the parties concerned determine the division of pensions at their discretion, they need to report the details, such as the division ratio, to the NPS.

§3. Insurance Coverage Period

193. The insurance coverage period means the period during which an insured person has maintained his/her entitlement and actually paid the contributions. This Act allows him/her to be exempted from the payment if there is an objective cause for which he/she cannot pay the contributions (Article 91 of this Act). The examples are the cases where a person is in suspension of business, unemployment or leave of absence; where a person is doing his military service; where a person is a student; where a person is confined in a correction facility; where a person is committed to a preventive custody facility or a medical treatment and custody facility; where a person's whereabouts are unknown for less than one year; where a person's income decreased as a result of a disaster or an accident; where a person fails to engage in income-earning activities; or as prescribed by Presidential Decree (*see* Article 60 of its Enforcement Decree). In principle, the period during which one's obligation to pay the contributions is exempted is not included in the insurance coverage period. Meanwhile, this Act presents an opportunity to make a postponed payment of the contributions for the period in which such contributions are not paid. It is to prevent the insurance coverage period from diminishing and the pension amount from decreasing for that reason. Accordingly, when an insured person pays the contributions later retroactively for the period during which one's obligation to pay the contributions was exempted, that period is included in the insurance coverage period (Article 92 of this Act).

194. In addition, this Act started to implement a system called an additionally included period (credit) in January 2008. This system acknowledges an additional period, even without payment of contributions, as long as a person meets certain requirements prescribed by the law to include the period. This allows him/her to acquire the entitlement for old-age pension or the amount of his/her old-age pension to increase as much. The requirements for and the length of the included period are as follows: first, Article 18(1) of this Act stipulates that six months will be added to the coverage period for a person who served in active duty service or a public interest service personnel who served after January 2008. However, they will not be added if the whole or part of his military service period was already included in the term of service pursuant to other laws, such as the Public Officials Pension Act, or if the contributions were paid during that period and such period was already acknowledged as the coverage period. Moreover, Article 19(1) of this Act provides that when a currently or formerly insured person with two or more children acquires entitlement to an old-age pension, an additional period will be added based on the number of children: if the number is two, twelve months will be added and if the number is three or higher, twelve months will be added for the first two kids and eighteen months for each additional child, up to fifty months. If both parents are currently or formerly insured, such additional period will be added only to one of the parents, as agreed by them. If the parents fail to reach an agreement, the additional period will be divided equally and be added to each parent's coverage period. Recently, a programme called 'unemployment credit' was introduced, which adds the period during which an insured person receives the job seeker's allowance under the Employment Insurance Act to the coverage period (Article 19(2) of this Act, enforced in July 2015). However, such period is limited to one year even if the allowance is received repeatedly. With regard to the period included in the coverage period, the insured person is deemed to be insured based on recognized income (half the amount of monthly wage converted from daily wage, which serves as the basis when calculating the job seeker's allowance pursuant to Article 45 of the Employment Insurance Act; the upper and lower limits of the recognized income are prescribed and announced by the Minister of Health and Welfare.) If a person wishes to enjoy the unemployment credit programme, he/she is obliged to pay the contributions based on his/her recognized income. In that case, he/she bears a quarter of the contributions, and the government bears three quarters.

Chapter 3. Disability Pension

§1. Beneficiaries

195. When a disability occurs to an insured person during the coverage period, disability pension is paid based on the degree of disability for as long as the disability persists. A disability eligible for disability pension refers to a physically or mentally unstable status despite having fully recovered from a disease or injury that occurred during the insurance coverage period. Here, a 'disease or injury that occurred during the insurance coverage period' means a case where the date of the first medical examination on the relevant disease occurs within the insurance coverage period, including a case where an insured person was unaware of the outbreak of a disease at the time he/she became insured (Article 67(1) of this Act). Therefore, even if a disability occurs during the coverage period, if its cause is a disease or injury that had developed prior to the subscription to the pension plan, then the insured person is not eligible for disability pension. On the other hand, if the insured person was not aware of the outbreak of such disease or injury at the time of joining the pension plan, he/she may be a beneficiary of disability pension (Supreme Court Decision No. 2011Du31178 dated 13 April 2012).

§2. Conditions

196. As a general rule, a disability should result from a disease or injury that occurred while an insured person is insured by the pension plan. In other words, there should be a causal relationship between the two. The Supreme Court judges that the factors to be considered to determine the causal relationship should be whether the disease or injury in question is the medical and objective cause of the disability. With this in mind, it is not sufficient to recognize the causal relationship simply because there is the likelihood that a disease or injury present before joining the pension plan may have led to the outbreak of the disability (Supreme Court Decision No. 2005Du16918 dated 28 July 2006).

197. If a person who sustains a disease or injury fails to recover completely even after one and a half years since the date of the first medical examination, the degree of disability is determined as of the date on which the one and a half years have passed or at the time when the disability can be confirmed within this period of one and a half years. However, if a person who was not entitled to receive disability pension on the date on which the one and a half years have passed later becomes entitled to disability pension before reaching age 60 because the disease or injury has worsened, the degree of disability is determined upon the request of the person as of the date of such request (Article 67(2) of this Act). Moreover, if a person whose entitlement to disability pension has terminated because his/her degree of disability is adjusted pursuant to Article 70(1) of this Act regains entitlement to disability pension before reaching the age of 61 due to a worsened disease or injury that he/she sustained at the time he/she acquired entitlement to the disability pension, then the degree of disability is determined upon the request of the person as of the date of such request (Article 67(3) of this Act). The degrees of disabilities are classified into four: first, second, third, and fourth degrees. The criteria for the classification and the examination of the extent of disability are set forth by the Presidential Decree (Article 67(5) of this Act; Article 46 of its Enforcement Decree).

§3. Pension Calculation

198. Disability benefits consist of disability pension and disability compensation. A person with a first-degree disability is entitled to receive the sum of basic pension amount and dependant's pension amount, and a person with a second-degree disability is entitled to receive the sum of basic pension amount and 80/100 of dependant's pension amount. A person with a third-degree disability is entitled to receive the sum of basic pension amount, and 60/100 of dependant's pension amount and a person with a fourth-degree disability is entitled to receive a lump-sum disability compensation equivalent to 225/100 of basic pension amount, and dependant's pension amount is not paid.

199. When a beneficiary of disability pension sustains another disability, the degree of disability is determined again by combining the extent of both former and latter disabilities, and his/her disability pension amount is determined accordingly (Article 69 of this Act). In addition, if a disability pension beneficiary's degree of disability changes, the pension amount changes according to the new degree of disability (Article 70 of this Act). Please note that the two cases are different. The former (adjustment due to overlapping disabilities) is for the beneficiaries of disability pension to whom another disability occurs from a cause different from that of the initial disability. On the other hand, the latter (adjustment of disability pension amount) is for the beneficiaries whose degree of disability had been confirmed but has worsened or relieved after. However, these do not apply to the beneficiaries aged 60 or older. In this case, when a beneficiary's degree of disability is re-examined, the severity of the disability is determined based on the date on which a disease or injury is completely recovered (Article 70(3) of this Act); if a disease or injury is not fully recovered, the severity of the disability is determined based on the date prescribed by the Presidential Decree, such as the last day of the month during which a cycle designated by the NPS according to the probability of changes in disability degree arrives (related to Article 70(1) of this Act), or the date on which a beneficiary requests for a change to his/her disability pension amount (related to Article 70(2) of this Act).

200. When a beneficiary of lump-sum disability compensation faces overlapping disabilities or an altered degree of disability, he/she is deemed to have received monthly pension amount equivalent to 40/100 of basic pension amount for sixty-seven months (Article 71 of this Act). This provision reflects the technical difficulties in adjusting the pension amount due to the overlapping disabilities or change of the degree of disability. A beneficiary of lump-sum disability compensation may begin to receive pension benefits after sixty-seven months elapse.

Chapter 4. Survivors Pension

§1. Beneficiaries

201. When an insured person of the national pension plan, a beneficiary of old-age pension, a person entitled to receive pension benefits (whose coverage period is ten years or more), or a beneficiary of disability pension with at least a second-degree disability dies, the family of the deceased is paid survivor's pension. However, if the person who died of a disease or injury had held the pension plan for less than one year, survivor's pension is paid only where such death is caused by a disease or injury which arose during the coverage period. If a person whose coverage period was less than ten years (and therefore yet to be entitled to receive the pension) dies of a disease, an injury or a disease resulting from such injury that arose during the coverage period within two years from the date of the first medical examination during the coverage period or from the date of the first medical examination within one year from the moment he/she lost his/her insured status, the family of the deceased is entitled to receive survivor's pension.

202. Survivors entitled to survivor's pension are the following persons whose livelihood is supported by a current or former insured person at the time the person dies: spouse, a child under age 18 or with at least a second-degree disability, a parent aged 61 or older or with at least a second-degree disability (including the parent of a spouse), grandchild under age 18 or with at least a second-degree disability, grandparent (including grandparent of a spouse) aged 61 or older or with at least a second-degree disability. Survivor's pension is paid only to the highest-ranked person in the order of priority as listed above. For instance, if the spouse's entitlement to a survivor's pension is suspended or terminated, the pension is paid to the child, who is the next in line. If there are two or more persons within the same ranking, the pension amount is equally divided among such survivors (Article 73 of this Act; Articles 40 and 48 of its Enforcement Decree).

§2. Conditions

203. According to Article 75(1) of this Act, one's entitlement to survivor's pension is terminated (i) if the beneficiary dies; (ii) if the beneficiary who is a spouse remarries; (iii) if the beneficiary who is a child or grandchild is adopted or whose adoption is dissolved; (iv) if the beneficiary who is a child or grandchild and who does not fall within at least a second-degree disability category reaches the age of 18; or (v) if the person who has acquired entitlement to a pension on the grounds of disability no longer qualifies as having at least a second-degree disability. Furthermore, a parent, grandchild, or grandparent's entitlement to survivor's pension terminates if a baby of a current or former insured person, who was a foetus at the time of the death of the current or former insured person, is born and thereby acquires the entitlement to survivor's pension (Article 75(2) of this Act).

204. Under Article 76(1) of this Act, survivor's pension is paid to a spouse who is the beneficiary of survivor's pension for three years from the time the spouse becomes entitled to such pension and then suspended until the spouse reaches the age of 55. However, if the beneficiary is with at least a second-degree disability, if the beneficiary has supported the livelihood of a current or former insured person's child under 18 or such person's child with at least a second-degree disability, or if the beneficiary is not engaged in income-earning activities prescribed by the Presidential Decree (the beneficiary's income-earning activities refer to activities generating income whether as an employee in a workplace or a business owner, where an amount obtained by dividing the aggregate of real estate rental income, business income, and earned income pursuant to the provisions of the Income Tax Act, by the number of months a person is engaged in an activity in a fiscal year concerned exceeds an amount calculated by converting the average of the standard monthly income of all pension subscribers as of the year-end of the previous year three years preceding the first year of the payment of pension benefits (KRW 1,791,955 in 2010). *See* Article 45 of its Enforcement Decree), the payment of such pension is not suspended.

§3. CALCULATION

205. The amount of survivor's pension is the sum of basic pension amount, calculated differently based on the coverage period of the deceased pursuant to Article 74 of this Act, and dependant's pension amount. However, when a beneficiary of old-age pension dies, the amount of survivor's pension cannot exceed the old-age pension amount paid to the deceased. In addition, Article 75 of this Act stipulates the reasons of termination of the entitlement to survivor's pension and Article 76 of this Act provides the requirements for the suspension of payment of survivor's pension to the spouse who is the beneficiary of survivor's pension.

Chapter 5. Lump-Sum Refund and Others

206. In principle, the national pension pays benefits on the assumption that the beneficiary contributes to the finances for a certain period of time upon the occurrence of risks, such as old age and death, and pension benefits are paid in instalments, instead of a lump-sum, to ensure consistent income for the beneficiaries. However, this Act has an exceptional lump-sum refund clause. A lump-sum refund is paid at the request of the person himself/herself or his/her bereaved family when a person whose coverage period is less than ten years reaches the age of 60 or when a person can no longer be insured by the NPS due to his/her death, loss of his/her nationality or overseas emigration. The amount of the refund is the total amount of contributions paid during the coverage period and the interest calculated at a certain rate (Article 77 of this Act).

207. When a current or former insured person dies but has no family as defined in Article 73 of this Act, a lump-sum death payment is made to the spouse, children, parents, grandchildren, grandparents, siblings, first cousins or closer collateral blood relatives of the deceased. However, the payment is not made to a person whose whereabouts are unknown as a result of abscondence from home or missing. In addition, the lump-sum death payment is given to a first cousin or closer collateral blood relative only if his/her livelihood is supported by a current or former insured person at the time of death of the insured person as prescribed by the Presidential Decree (Article 80 of this Act).

Part IX. Handicapped Persons

Chapter 1. Social Integration

§1. Significance and Purpose of This Act

208. The Act on Welfare of Persons with Disabilities is significant in that it presents ways of ultimate social rehabilitation so that persons with disabilities can contribute to social integration as a member of society by preventing disabilities from occurring *ex ante* and providing special measures for rehabilitation and independent living of persons with disabilities *ex post.*

209. To do so, this Act aims to contribute to social integration through the welfare and the promotion of participation in social activities of persons with disabilities by clarifying the responsibilities of the central and local governments for ensuring their decent life and the rights, planning and implementing comprehensive welfare measures for them through a variety of programmes related to the prevention of disability from occurring, medical care, education, vocational rehabilitation, and improvement of living environment for them, and contributing to their stable livelihood by determining matters necessary for their independent living, protection and payment of allowances (Article 1 of this Act). The constitutional grounds of this Act include the right to be assured of human worth and dignity and the right to pursue happiness (Article 10 of the Constitution), the right to equality (Article 11) and the right to be entitled to a life worthy of human beings (Article 34). In particular, Article 34(5) of the Constitution stipulates that any citizen who is incapable of leading a life due to his/her physical disability, disease, old age or other reasons should be protected by the nation as prescribed by the law, emphasizing the nation's duty to assure the right of persons with disabilities to live a life worthy of human beings.

§2. Fundamental Principles and Care Structure

I. Fundamental Principles of Social Integration

210. The fundamental principle of the Act on Welfare of Persons with Disabilities is to achieve social integration through complete social participation and equality of persons with disabilities, who face social constraints in their life due to their disabilities (Article 3 of this Act). Persons with disabilities should be respected with their human dignity and value, and be treated as such (Article 4(1) of this Act). In other words, the fundamental principle of this Act is to establish the measures of social consideration to make persons with disabilities enjoy an equal social life with persons without disabilities and build social integration in which they can lead a normal life.

II. Realization of Participation (Welfare Benefits) and Equality (Prohibition of Discrimination)

211. 'Complete social participation and equality' is essential in order to realize the principle of social integration of persons with disabilities. In other words, disabilities welfare benefits should be provided to allow persons with disabilities to participate in social activities, and discrimination against disabilities must be prohibited in all areas. Such participation (welfare benefits) and equality (prohibition of discrimination) are complementary to each other and contribute to social integration together. To ensure both, this Act specifically stipulates the participation right to participation of persons with disabilities and the discrimination against them.

212. Persons with disabilities have a right to participate in activities of all fields, including political, economic, social, cultural fields, as a member of a nation and a society. Also, they have a right to preferentially participate in the policymaking processes related to them (Article 4 of this Act). No person with a disability should be discriminated against, or no one should discriminate against persons with disabilities, in any area of political, economic, social or cultural life due to one's disability (Article 8(1) of this Act).

III. Comprehensive Care Structure

213. The laws to implement the principle of social integration and to realize decent lives of persons with disabilities have taken in a multi-functional and comprehensive care structure.

214. The Act on Welfare of Persons with Disabilities is the framework act with regard to the welfare of persons with disabilities, and more concrete laws to realize the goal (i.e., participation and equality) that this Act aims to have been established in a multifaceted manner. The laws ensuring disabilities welfare benefits for the promotion of participation include the Act on the Guarantee of Promotion of Convenience of Persons with Disabilities, Elderly People, Pregnant Women, Etc. to assure such persons' access to facilities and information; the Act on Promotion of the Transportation Convenience of Mobility Disadvantaged Persons to assure such persons' mobility right; the Act on Special Education for persons with Disabilities, Etc. to provide a consolidated environment of education; and the Act on the Employment Promotion and Vocational Rehabilitation of Persons with Disabilities as well as the Act on the Facilitation of Entrepreneurial Activities of Persons with

Disabilities to promote employment and business start-ups. Moreover, the Act on the Prohibition of Discrimination against Persons with Disabilities, Remedy against Infringement of Their Rights, Etc. (hereinafter 'the Act on the Prohibition of Discrimination') was established to prohibit discrimination and ensure equality.

Chapter 2. Financial Allowances for the Handicapped

§1. Beneficiaries

215. The concept of disability should be clearly defined to determine the welfare beneficiaries under the Act on Welfare of Persons with Disabilities. The approach to the concept started from individual, medical and pathological perspectives and changed to the perspective of social integration.

216. The persons with disabilities protected under this Act refer to those whose daily life or social activity is substantially constrained by their physical or mental disability over a long period of time (Article 2 of this Act). This Act enumerates concrete criteria to judge disability: it presents classifications of disabilities, such as physical disability, brain lesions, visual impairment, hearing impairment, speech and language disorder, intellectual disability, autistic disorder, mental disability, renal disorder, cardiac disorder, respiratory disorder, hepatopathy, facial disorder, intestinal/urinary disorder and epileptic disorder (*see* Table 1 of the Enforcement Decree of this Act for the details).

§2. Benefits

217. The system of disabilities welfare benefits may be classified into the system under this Act and the system under the comprehensive laws on disabilities welfare benefits.

I. Welfare Benefits under This Act

218. First are protective measures. The central and local governments should investigate the causes of disabilities to prevent them, and consider policies needed to detect and treat disabilities early. Moreover, the governments should seek measures to prevent traffic accidents, industrial accidents, drug addiction and environmental pollution as they are some of the causes of disabilities (Article 17 of this Act). Second are rehabilitation measures. The central and local governments should establish measures, such as medical rehabilitation (Article 18), educational rehabilitation (Article 20), vocational rehabilitation(Article 21), and rehabilitation counselling and admission to institutions (Article 34). Third are measures to support one's self-subsistence. The central and local governments should provide measures to allow persons with disabilities to be independent and lead normal lives, such as business loans (Article 41), business support (Article 42), supply of self-reliance training expenses (Article 43) and preferential purchase of goods produced at welfare facilities for persons with disabilities (Article 44). Fourth are measures for education for children and support. The welfare services agencies for persons with disabilities provide the education expenses for the children who are supported by persons with disabilities and the children who are persons with disabilities (Article

38). In addition, the central and local governments may provide disability allowances as a means of living subsidy, taking into account the degree of disability and economic status of the persons with disabilities (Article 49). Furthermore, allowance for children with disabilities and guardian allowance may be paid to a protector or a guardian taking care of children with disabilities (Article 50). Fifth are other measures, such as medical expenses. The welfare services agencies for persons with disabilities may pay medical expenses of low-income persons with disabilities who are acknowledged to have difficulty in bearing medical expenses (Article 36).

II. Welfare Benefits under Comprehensive Laws on Disabilities Welfare Benefits

219. Below is the welfare benefits system to ensure participation and equality for the social integration of persons with disabilities in a detailed manner.

220. First are the laws assuring the rights to welfare benefits to ensure participation. Examples are promoting employment under the Act on the Employment Promotion and Vocational Rehabilitation of Persons with Disabilities, assuring access to facilities and information under the Act on the Guarantee of Promotion of Convenience of Persons with Disabilities, Elderly People, Pregnant Women, Etc. and guaranteeing mobility right under the Act on Promotion of the Transportation Convenience of Mobility Disadvantaged Persons. Second are measures against discrimination to realize equality. The Act on the Prohibition of Discrimination, for instance, stipulates a variety of benefits related thereto.

III. Ensuring Participation: Rights to Welfare Benefits

A. Employment Promotion

221. The Act on the Employment Promotion and Vocational Rehabilitation of Persons with Disabilities stipulates mandatory employment quota system for persons with disabilities, which requires the central and local governments and private companies to hire a certain ratio of persons with disabilities. The mandatory quota system secures employment opportunity of persons with disabilities who have ability and intent to work, thereby promoting vocational independence of persons with disabilities and their welfare. It is an institutionalized system proving that employers are also responsible for social solidarity as a member of society, and for cooperating for social security against disability, which is one of the social risks. Under the quota system, the central and local governments are required to hire persons with disabilities for at least 3.2% of their prescribed number of public officials and persons hired through open employment. The maximum age limit for applying for such open employment is extended for persons with disabilities: by three years for persons with severe disabilities and by two years for other persons with disabilities, respectively (Article 27). Companies are also imposed on such duty to hire persons with disabilities to a certain extent. Any business owner who employs at least fifty workers is required to employ persons with disabilities to fill at least a certain ratio as determined in the Presidential Decree up to 5% of the total number of workers (Article 28 of this Act; Article 25 of its Enforcement Decree). This system promotes and forces the employment of persons with disabilities by granting employment incentives to the owners who have hired persons with disabilities and imposing the contributory charge to the owners who have failed to do so.

222. Business owners have their freedom of business and freedom of contract, under which they are free to determine with whom to conclude employment contracts. With this in mind, this mandatory employment quota system inevitably creates a conflict with their freedom. The issue here is whether the quota system infringes business owners' freedom of contract and freedom of economic activity and whether it is against the principle of equality because the contributory charge is not imposed on the central and local governments.

B. Right to Access

223. The right to access means 'a right of persons with disabilities to use facilities and equipment used by persons without disabilities and have free access to information to be assured of the right to pursue dignity, value and happiness as a human being' (Article 4 of the Act on the Guarantee of Promotion of Convenience of Persons with Disabilities, Elderly People, Pregnant Women, Etc.). This right has also deemed a right to guarantee other rights (e.g., right to receive education).

224. The access rights for persons with disabilities may be classified into 'right of access to information', which is about receiving all the services needed for expression of opinion and use of information, including communication, sign language interpreting, subtitles, braille and audiobooks, 'right of facility use', which is about receiving convenience in public facilities and other places, and 'right of mobility', which is about using means of transportation, including bus, subway and taxi.

C. Right to Mobility

225. Persons with disabilities should be guaranteed mobility through means of transportation to have a job, receive education and lead ordinary political, economic, social and cultural life. It is safe to say that their right to mobility is a prerequisite for them to enjoy other rights. Their right of mobility refers to 'a right of persons with disabilities to use all means of transportation, passenger facilities, and roads used by non-disadvantaged persons safely, conveniently, and without discrimination, to be assured of the right to pursue dignity, value and happiness as a human being' (Article 3 of the Act on Promotion of the Transportation Convenience of Mobility Disadvantaged Persons). Mobility of persons with disabilities is a concept that includes their movements between places indoor and outdoor, but the right of mobility, specifically regulates transportation, passenger facilities, and roads.

226. On 22 January 2001, a person with disabilities was killed, and another person was injured in an accident in which a metal pin of a vertical lift installed in Oido Station in Seoul Metropolitan Subway Line 4 was cut, which caused the lift to fall. After this accident, disabled groups started vigorous movements to assure the rights of persons with disabilities to use public transportation such as subway and bus.

IV. Disability Pension

227. The Act on Pensions for Persons with Disabilities was established on 12 April 2010 to support stable lives of persons with severe disabilities, who face difficulty in leading a life due to their disabilities (Article 1).

228. The beneficiary of disability pension is a person with severe disabilities aged 18 or more, whose recognized amount of income is lower than the amount publicly announced by the Minister of Health and Welfare determined by taking into account his/her income, property, the standard of living and the nation's inflation rate (Article 4).

229. Disability pension consists of 'basic allowance', which is paid to cover the income decreased as a result of loss or significant reduction of work ability, and 'additional allowance', which is paid to cover in full or in part the cost incurred due to disability (Article 5). The amount of basic allowance follows the standard pension benefits publicly announced pursuant to Article 9(3) of the Basic Pension Act. (If the standard pension benefits are not available, the amount calculated based on the basic allowance amount of the previous year by reflecting the national consumer price inflation rate as prescribed in the Presidential Decree and publicly announced by the Minister of Health and Welfare.) (In case both the beneficiary and his/her spouse receive a basic allowance, each basic allowance amount will be reduced by 20/100 as prescribed in Article 6(3).) Also, the amount of additional allowance is a fixed monthly amount, and it is determined pursuant to the Presidential Decree taking into consideration the income levels of the beneficiary and his/her spouse as well as additional costs incurred due to disabilities (Article 7).

230. In consideration of financial conditions of local governments, disability pension may be paid by the central government, or by the government of a metropolitan city, a province, a special self-governing city, a special self-governing province, or a Si/Gun/Gu (city, county, district), as prescribed in the Presidential Decree (Article 21). The central and local governments should make best effort to manage disability pension to a sufficient level to support stable lives of persons with severe disabilities and promote their welfare and are responsible for raising the fund on an annual basis (Article 3).

V. Finance and Management

231. The payments of medical expenses, educational expenses for children, self-reliance training expenses, disability allowances, allowance for children with disabilities, guardian allowance, support for assistance services such as an activity assistant, supply of auxiliary appliances for persons with disabilities, support and promotion of companies manufacturing auxiliary appliances for persons with disabilities, and the expenses related to the establishment of welfare facilities for persons with disabilities by the central and/or local governments under the Act on Welfare of Persons with Disabilities are to be made by the central and local governments, but the governments may ask the welfare services agencies for persons with disabilities to make such payments. The ratio of the costs to be borne by the central and local governments is as prescribed in the Enforcement Decree of the Act on the Budgeting and Management of Subsidies (Article 79 of the Act on Welfare of Persons with Disabilities, Article 42 of its Enforcement Decree).

232. The central and local governments under the Act on Welfare of Persons with Disabilities are responsible for the measures related to the protection of persons with disabilities (Article 9(1) of this Act). Accordingly, governments may establish welfare facilities for persons with disabilities. Private organizations are also allowed to establish such welfare facilities.

233. The supervisory authority over the welfare facilities for persons with disabilities is on the central or local governments. In other words, the welfare services agencies for persons with disabilities guide and supervise the operation of those who establish and operate welfare facilities for persons with disabilities as well as the realities of human rights of the users of the facilities. Also, they may order them to brief on the facilities or submit relevant documents, when necessary, or have a public official under its jurisdiction conduct an investigation or examination on the operations, books, and other documents of the facilities and ask questions to the persons concerned. According to the results of such supervision or investigation, they may issue an order to improve the facilities, suspend their operations, replace the head of the facilities, or shut down the facilities (Articles 61 and 62).

234. Furthermore, Policy Coordination Committee for Persons with Disabilities has been created to establish comprehensive welfare policies for persons with disabilities, to coordinate different opinions of the Ministries concerned and to monitor and evaluate the execution of such policies (Article 11).

Part X. Minimum Income Benefit

Chapter 1. Overview

§1. Significance

235. With an aim to provide customized benefits based on specific criteria for each type of benefits, the amended Act on National Basic Living Security stipulates that an eligible recipient may receive all or part of benefits prescribed in Article 7(1)1 through 7(1)7 depending on the recipient's needs. To do so, the criteria and payment for benefits are made by each type, which requires that each benefit type be managed by different competent central administrative agencies. The types of benefits are livelihood benefits, housing benefits, medical benefits, education benefits, childbirth benefits, funeral benefits and self-sufficiency benefits (Article 7(1) of this Act). These benefits may be paid by social welfare facilities (Article 32 of this Act), in which case the heads of the facilities should pay the benefits above the minimum level as determined (Article 33 of this Act).

§2. Significance and Current Status of Public Assistance

236. The term 'public assistance' means a system in which the central and local governments take responsibility of supporting citizens who are unable to maintain basic living standards or who live in financial hardships so that they can sustain a minimum livelihood and stand on their feet (Article 3(3) of the Framework Act on Social Security). The prime goal of the income security system, including social insurance, is to provide fixed and standard benefits in the event of general risks in life, such as disease, injury, disability, death, old age, occupational accident and unemployment, thereby maintaining the livelihoods of beneficiaries and their families and preventing them from being impoverished. However, there are quite a number of cases in which an unexpected event occurs, and even if the event is subject to the benefits, the benefits are not paid because the requirements for their payments are not satisfied. Public assistance is a system designed to deal with such cases where citizens face difficulties in maintaining a minimum level of living standards. In other words, it serves as the very last safety net of people's life.

237. The statutes related to public assistance mainly include the Act on National Basic Living Security and the Medical Care Assistance Act. Prior to the enactment of the former, there was a law called the Livelihood Protection Act enacted in 1961.

However, it severely restricted the persons subject to protection (old and infirm people aged 65 or more, children under 18, pregnant women, those unable to work due to a fatal disease or a mental/physical disability), the criteria to determine the beneficiaries were not made into the law, and the benefits were far from ensuring the minimum level of living standards. In other words, the Livelihood Protection Act was very insufficient to be a public assistance system to respond to the distressed life of the citizens. Following the Asian Financial Crisis in 1997, the modification of the nation's social security net emerged as the main challenge in our society, and this led to the significant improvement to the Livelihood Protection Act. The Act on National Basic Living Security was enacted accordingly and came into force as of 1 October 2000. Still, the new law had drawbacks that needed to be corrected. For instance, one may receive various types of benefits when his/her recognized amount of income is equal to or lower than the minimum cost of living, but one is excluded from support even if he/she needs to be protected when he/she is not recognized as an eligible recipient. Accordingly, an amendment of the Act on National Basic Living Security was passed by the National Assembly in December 2014 (enforced on 1 July 2015), which changed the basic living security system into more effective, efficient and customized anti-poverty policies in an attempt to expand the eligible recipients and to reinforce poverty prevention function by introducing a benefit structure that is more favourable to those who work.

238. As for the beneficiaries of medical assistance, their range is expanded, pursuant to Article 3 of the Act on National Basic Living Security, beyond the eligible recipients under the Act, and a separate fund called the Medical Assistance Fund is established to cover the medical care expenses. In this regard, since the matters related to medical assistance are distinguished from those defined by the Act on National Basic Living Security, they are regulated by a separate law.

239. The number of beneficiaries under the Act on National Basic Living Security is on a gradual decrease from 2010, and overall, it is around 2%–3% of the entire population.

Chapter 2. Beneficiaries

§1. Eligible Recipients of Public Assistance

240. The recipients of the three benefits are determined based on the requirements of obligatory provider and recognized amount of income. The former requires that a recipient should not have an obligatory provider (i.e., the person responsible for rendering support to an eligible recipient), or should have an obligatory provider but the provider is unable to support the recipient, or the recipient is unable to receive support from the provider. An obligatory provider being unable to support the recipient refers to cases in which the provider's income and the property are below the level prescribed by the Presidential Decree in consideration of the standard median income level, in which the provider provides supports, in his/her residential place, to a lineal ascendant, or to a lineal descendant who is a severely disabled person as prescribed by Article 2(1) of the Act on Pensions for Persons with Disabilities, or in which the Minister of Health and Welfare determines the provider unable to support the recipient due to the provider's disease, education and household characteristics (Article 8-2(1) of this Act). The recipient being unable to receive support from the provider refers to cases in which the provider has been drafted or called up into the army pursuant to the Military Service Act, in which he/she has emigrated overseas, or in which he/she is in prison, detention centre or medical treatment and custody facility (Article 8-2(2) of this Act).

241. In addition, to become an eligible recipient, his/her recognized amount of income should be below the criteria for selection per type of benefits. The criteria are usually an amount equivalent to a certain percentage or higher of the standard median income. The recognized amount of income of an individual household is calculated so that assistance facilities can make decisions and payments of the benefits. It is calculated by subtracting the amount of various expenditures from the actual income of the household (Article 6-3 of this Act). Meanwhile, the criteria for selection for each type of benefits are publicly announced by the Minister of Health and Welfare or the head of the competent central administrative agency by 1 August of each year after going through the deliberation and resolution by the Central Livelihood Security Committee (Article 6 of this Act). The minimum security level for each type of benefits is also determined by using the same procedure as the procedure for selecting the eligible recipients.

242. An eligible recipient of childbirth benefits and funeral benefits must be an eligible recipient of at least one of livelihood, housing and medical benefits while an eligible recipient of any of the benefits can be a beneficiary of self-sufficiency benefits. These benefits are not independent because the eligibility for these benefits is determined by his/her eligibility for other benefits. The details of housing benefits are prescribed by other laws, so their eligible recipients are determined according to the relevant laws.

243. Please note that a person may be deemed an eligible recipient even when he/she is not a beneficiary of any of the above seven types of benefits. He/she may be deemed so if the person lives in financial hardships, and the Minister of Health and Welfare or the head of the competent central administrative agency determines that he/she needs all or part of the benefits prescribed in this Act for a certain period of time (Article 14-2 of this Act).

§2. Determination of the Recipients

244. In order to become an eligible recipient of livelihood benefits, he/she must fulfil the requirement of obligatory provider and have his/her recognized amount of income below the amount determined in the criteria for selection for livelihood benefits, which is at least 30/100 of the standard median income (Article 8(2). Note: The criteria may be set up differently in case the payment of livelihood benefits is entrusted to assistance facilities under Article 32(Article 8(4)). In addition, to become an eligible recipient of education benefits, his/her recognized amount of income should be lower than the amount determined in the criteria for selection for education benefits, which is at least 50/100 of the standard median income (Article 12(3) of this Act). The requirement of obligatory provider has been deleted for education benefits in order to connect and integrate with the educational support programme under the Elementary and Secondary Education Act (Article 12-2 of this Act). Moreover, to become an eligible recipient of medical benefits, he/she must fulfil the requirement of obligatory provider and have his/her recognized amount of income below the amount determined in the criteria for selection for medical benefits, which is at least 40/100 of the standard median income (Article 12-3(2) of this Act). A beneficiary pursuant to Article 3 of the Medical Care Assistance Act constitutes an eligible recipient of medical benefits. Furthermore, the criteria for selection for housing benefits are at least 43/100 of the standard median income (Article 5(1) of the Housing Benefits Act).

Chapter 3. Conditions

245. An eligible recipient, his/her relative, or any other relevant person need to file an application to the head of the competent Si/Gun/Gu (city, county, district) if he/she wishes to receive the benefits under the jurisdiction of the Ministry of Health and Welfare pursuant to the Act on National Basic Living Security (Article 21(1) of this Act). However, not all recipients are able to send the application; hence, public officials in charge of social welfare are allowed to apply ex officio on behalf of the recipients who reside in his/her competent area with their consent. In this case, the consent of the relevant eligible recipient may be deemed an application filed by the recipient him/herself (Article 21(2) of this Act).

246. When the application is received, assistance facilities should ask their public officials in charge of social welfare to conduct an investigation on the recipient's income, property, matters related to support relations and his/her household characteristics in order to gather information necessary to make the decision on and payment of the benefits (Article 22 of this Act). Assistance facilities should conduct a follow-up investigation regularly, at least once a year, to confirm the above items. The details described above in relation to the application for the benefits apply *mutatis mutandis* to the lowest-income earners (Article 21(1) of this Act).

247. Meanwhile, the procedures for assistance for educational expenses under the Elementary and Secondary Education Act apply *mutatis mutandis* to the application for and payment of education benefits (Article 12(4) of this Act). The application procedures for housing benefits and medical benefits are determined as prescribed by the relevant laws.

Chapter 4. Amount of the Benefit

248. The purpose of public assistance is to provide a sufficient level of benefits to achieve the goal of helping the citizens sustain a minimum level of living standards. To this end, limitations are imposed on the actual amount of livelihood benefits, which play a fundamental role in ensuring basic living security, saying that the amount should not be below the selection criteria of livelihood benefits, including the recognized amount of income (Article 8(3) of this Act). Moreover, the minimum security level of each type of benefits is determined and publicly announced by the Minister of Health and Welfare or the head of the competent central administrative agency, but it must go through the deliberation and resolution by the Central Livelihood Security Committee to keep and improve the adequacy and rationality of the minimum security level (Article 20(2)3 of this Act).

§1. Livelihood Benefits

249. Livelihood benefits are provided to the recipients as clothing, food, fuel costs and other cash and goods necessary for their daily lives so that they can maintain their livelihood (Article 8 of this Act). The principal mode of payment is cash, but if it is unable or deemed inappropriate to provide the benefits in cash, then they may be provided in kind (Article 9(1) of this Act. The criteria for selection and level of benefits are explained in detail in the following sections IV-1 and IV-3). The cash and goods are in principle paid directly to the recipients on a regular (monthly) basis, but when the benefits are paid via an assistance facility or another family who was entrusted to do the job, such facility or family may provide the benefits to the recipients and should check on a regular basis whether the recipients have received the benefits (Article 9(2) and 9(3) of this Act). Moreover, livelihood benefits are in principle provided in the residence of a recipient. However, if he/she does not have residence, or if the purpose of assistance is unattainable therein even if he/she has a residence, or if he/she so wishes, the payment of the benefits may be entrusted to an assistance facility under Article 32 or another family (Article 10 of this Act).

250. Livelihood benefits may be provided conditionally for a person able to work, which is called 'conditional benefits.' In other words, a person who has the ability to work may receive the benefits on the condition that he/she engages in work needed for his/her self-support (Article 9(5) of this Act). A recipient of the conditional benefits refers to a recipient aged between 18 and 64. Articles 7 and 8 of its Enforcement Decree provide in detail whether a person is recognized to have the ability to work, or whether a person is able to work but have difficulty in taking part in self-support work due to some reasons.

§2. Housing Benefits

251. Housing benefits are to cover rental fees, maintenance and repair expenses and other cash and goods necessary for the recipient's residential stability (Article

11(1) of this Act). Rental fees are about paying monthly rent or lending the key money. Maintenance and repair expenses are provided for a recipient who owns a house and lives therein, or who lives in a house owned by another person free of charge. As the competent authorities have changed to the Ministry of Land, Infrastructure, and Transport, the matters required for housing benefits are prescribed separately by other laws (Article 11(2) of this Act).

§3. Education Benefits

252. Education benefits are offered in the form of admission fees, tuition fees, stationery expenses and other cash and goods to those who are in or start an elementary school, middle school, high school, special school, or a school similar to schools listed above under the Elementary and Secondary Education Act, or a school-type lifelong educational establishment under the Lifelong Education Act (Article 12 of this Act). The competent authorities for education benefits have changed to the Ministry of Education, so the procedures for assistance for educational expenses under the Elementary and Secondary Education Act apply *mutatis mutandis* to the payment of education benefits (Article 12(4) of this Act).

§4. Medical Benefits

253. Medical benefits aim to provide the recipient with various physical examinations and medical treatment needed for him/her to lead a healthy life (Article 12-3(1) of this Act). The matters necessary for medical benefits other than the criteria for selection of medical benefits are prescribed separately by the Medical Care Assistance Act (Article 12-3(3) of this Act). The types of benefits under the Medical Care Assistance Act include consultation and medical examination for disease, injury and childbirth; supply of medicine and materials for medical treatment; treatment, surgery, and other remedies; prevention and rehabilitation; hospitalization; nursing; transfer to other hospitals and other measures for accomplishing medical purposes. The expenses for medical benefits are covered by the Medical Assistance Fund in full or in part. In the latter case, the remaining expenses are covered by the recipient him/herself.

§5. Childbirth Benefits

254. Childbirth benefits are paid to a recipient who receives at least one of livelihood, housing and medical benefits, aiming to provide maternity service and measures and protection required before and after childbirth (Article 13(1) of this Act). The payment of the benefits may be entrusted to a medical institution designated by an assistance facility as prescribed by the Ordinance of the Ministry of Health and Welfare. The necessary cash and goods are provided to the recipient, his/her household or a person equivalent to his/her household as provided by the Ordinance (Article 13(2) and 13(3) of this Act).

§6. Funeral Benefits

255. Funeral benefits are offered when a recipient receiving at least one of livelihood, housing and medical benefits has deceased to cover post-mortem examinations, transport of the corpse, and cremation or interment and other funeral-related matters. The principle is to pay the funeral expenses to the person who holds a funeral in cash, but if it is unable or deemed inappropriate to provide the benefits in cash, then they may be provided in kind (Article 14 of this Act).

§7. Self-Sufficiency Benefits

256. Self-sufficiency benefits are provided for the recipients under the Act on National Basic Living Security in the form of payment or loan of money or provision or lease of goods required for self-support; support for improving vocational ability and acquiring skills necessary for self-support; provision of information, such as for job placement; provision of employment opportunities for self-support; lease of facilities and equipment necessary for self-support; support for business start-up, such as entrepreneurship education, skills training, and technical and management guidance; and assistance for the formation of assets necessary for self-support (Article 15 of this Act).

257. To promote one's self-support, assistance facilities (Article 19) are able to provide support for the establishment and management of self-support companies (Article 18), provide support for companies that hire the beneficiaries and persons belonging to the lowest-income bracket (Article 18-2), accumulate self-support fund (Article 18-3), support the beneficiaries and lowest-income earners to build assets (Article 18-4), and provide education and training (Article 18-5).

Part XI. Claims and Adjudications

258. The requirements and procedures for each scheme vary; please refer to the specific part of the chapter relevant to the topic of your interest for detailed information.

Part XII. Child Welfare Act

Chapter 1. Significance and Principles of the Child Welfare Act

259. In general, the rights of children rest on the United Nations Convention on the Rights of the Child. This Convention lays down the basic ideology that 'the best interests of children' must be the primary concern, and it includes a number of rights of children, such as respect for the views of the child, freedom of expression, freedom of association and other civil rights, parent's main responsibility and state assistance for bringing up their children, protection from abuse and exploitation, right to social security, protection from economic exploitation and harmful labour and right to juvenile justice. Child welfare, in a broad sense, includes such rights of children. This Convention was adopted in 1989 in commemoration of the thirtieth anniversary of the United Nations Declaration of the Rights of the Child, and South Korea ratified it in 1991. Therefore, it should be noted that this Convention has the same effect as Korea's domestic laws.

260. Korea's Child Welfare Act aims to ensure the welfare of children so that they can be born healthy and brought up happily and safely (Article 1 of this Act). To achieve this goal, this Act introduces the following basic principles: first, a child should grow up without experiencing any kind of discrimination based upon his/her or his/her parents' gender, age, religion, social status, wealth, disabilities, place of birth, race, and other factors. Second, a child should grow up happily in a stable family environment for the full and harmonious development of personality. Third, the interests of a child should be considered preferentially in all activities concerning a child.

261. In the end, the child welfare under this Act means all the activities done by the central and local governments as well as the entire society to support children and their families so that such goal and principles can be realized, and it refers to 'the economic, social and emotional support provided to children for the creation of basic conditions for children to enjoy a happy life and to grow up and develop harmoniously' (Article 3(2) of this Act). Articles 4 and 5 of this Act define the responsibilities of the State, the local governments, the protectors and all the citizens. However, it is inevitable that the child protection by the state may come into conflict with a parent's parental rights for their child. Therefore, the head of a competent local government should, when deemed necessary for the child's welfare, request the court to restrict the exercise of the parental rights or sentence the loss of the parental rights in a case where a person with parental rights of a child is found to have abused such rights or committed significant misconducts or where there are other serious reasons for which such parental rights cannot be exercised (Article 18 of this Act).

262. The Child Welfare Act is, in its nature, a law ensuring the welfare of children in general. It is not made only for children who need special protection. However, unfortunately, this Act lacks the characteristics to be considered as a general law encompassing the universal child welfare from birth to the growth of a child. For instance, the welfare covering the pregnancy, birth and infant care aiming to maintain and promote the health of mothers and infants is mainly regulated by the Mother and Child Health Act. Also, the welfare related to the protection of mind and body and the education of infants (i.e., child care) is primarily governed by the Infant Care Act. In addition, the detailed welfare programmes for children with disabilities are mainly regulated by the Act on Welfare of Persons with Disabilities. With these in mind, it shows that the range of children that need to be protected under the Child Welfare Act is quite limited. This Act has limitations that the welfare measures thereunder are established and implemented in order to protect the victims of child abuse and the children engaging in delinquent acts.

263. Lately, as child abuse crimes have become a social problem, the Act on Special Cases concerning the Punishment, etc. of Child Abuse Crimes was enacted. It is to strengthen punishment on persons committing child abuse crimes and to take urgent measures and protect the victims when child abuse crimes occur because abusive actions against children leave permanent scars on their emotional and physical health at their growth stage.

Chapter 2. Persons Subject to Protection

264. The Child Welfare Act protects children below the age of 18 (Article 3(1) of this Act). This Act stipulates the welfare system for children in general and prescribes measures for children who are in particular need of protection or support. A child who needs protection is referred to as 'a child subject to protection', which means that a child who has no protector or is separated from a protector, or whose protector is unsuitable for or incapable of raising them because, for instance, the protector abuses the child (Article 3(4) of this Act). In addition, a child who lacks basic conditions for harmonious and healthy growth and therefore needs social, economic and emotional support is called 'a child subject to support'. A child subject to support is included as part of a person subject to protection (Article 3(5) of this Act). The central and local governments are responsible for establishing and implementing systematic policies to promote the rights and interests of the children subject to protection and the children subject to support (Article 4(2) of this Act).

265. The role of parents and family is crucial for the healthy and safe upbringing of a child. That is why this Act includes children and their protectors as persons subject to protection. A protector means a person with parental rights, a guardian, a person who protects, raises and educates a child or who is responsible for such duties, or a person who actually protects and supervises a child for the reasons related to business or employment of a person with parental rights (Article 3(3) of this Act).

266. Moreover, this Act does not take one's nationality as a requirement for protection, so a stateless child or a child of an unregistered foreigner is subject to this Act.

Chapter 3. Categories and Substance of Benefits

267. A child grows up as he/she receives services required in each developmental stage in the boundary of the family from the moment he/she was born until he/she reaches 18 years old. In this sense, all children are socially vulnerable and therefore need to be protected. However, the current Act on Child Welfare offers benefits to provide a limited range of services to protect the children who need protection or assistance instead of providing universal services needed in each developmental stage.

§1. Prevention of and Measures Against Child Abuse

I. Measures for Child Subject to Protection

268. Article 15 of this Act stipulates that a mayor, a governor, or the head of a Si/Gun/Gu (city, county, district) should take following protective measures for the best interests of the child if he/she finds a child subject to protection within his/her jurisdiction or has received a protector's request: (i) having a public official in charge or a child commissioner provide counselling or guidance to a child subject to protection or his/her protector; (ii) taking necessary measures so that a protector or a relative who wishes to raise the child by proxy can protect and raise the child at his/her home; (iii) sending the child to a foster home run by a person who wishes to protect the child; (iv) putting the child subject to protection into a child welfare facility suitable for the protective measures; (v) hospitalizing or enrolling a child subject to protection in a specialized hospital or a care centre, for special medical care or recuperation, if the child has suffered from drug or alcohol addiction, emotional, behavioural or developmental disorder, or sexual violence; and (vi) taking measures necessary for adoption under the Act on Special Cases concerning Adoption (Article 15(1) of this Act).

269. A mayor, a governor, or the head of a Si/Gun/Gu (city, county, district) may take measures mentioned in (iii) through (vi) for a child subject to protection for whom the measures mentioned in (i) and (ii) are unsuitable. In such case, the relevant child must go through counselling, medical check-up, psychological test and an examination on his/her family background prior to taking protective measures mentioned in (iii) through (v) (Article 15(2) of this Act, to be enforced as of 23 March 2018). Furthermore, when deemed necessary, a child subject to protection may be provisionally sent to and protected by a temporary child welfare facility (Article 52(1)2 of this Act), a suitable foster home, or a person deemed appropriate prior to taking protective measures mentioned in (iii) through (vi) for the child. During this period, the relevant child must go through counselling, medical check-up, psychological test and an examination on his/her family background, and their results should be taken into consideration when taking appropriate protective measures (Article 15(5) of this Act, to be enforced as of 23 March 2018).

270. A mayor, a governor, or the head of a Si/Gun/Gu (city, county, district) should consider appropriate measures of prevention against families of children who are likely to cause trouble, such as drug or alcohol addiction, and emotional, behavioural or developmental disorder, within his/her jurisdiction (Article 15(6) of this Act). Moreover, he/she should check the criminal record of a person who wishes to provide a foster home to protect a child. Also, the head of a foster home supporting centre may request the relevant mayor, governor, or head of a Si/Gun/Gu (city, county, district) to cooperate with him/her in taking measures, such as confirming the identity of a foster care child, a person who wishes to provide a foster home to protect a child and parents of the foster care child (Article 15(8) through 15(10) of this Act).

271. The Child Welfare Act also provides protective measures, allowing a claim to restrict the exercise of the parental rights or sentence the loss of the parental rights pursuant to Article to be filed to the court or allowing the child to appoint his/her guardian when a child is abused by a person with parental rights (Articles 18 through 21 of this Act).

272. A mayor, a governor, or the head of a Si/Gun/Gu (city, county, district) may check the care situation of the child subject to protection protected under the above paragraph 268 (ii) through (vi) every year. Based on the inspection results, if he/she finds that the well-being of the child needs to be protected, or that the measures put in place are not adequate, he/she should change the protective measures without delay (Article 15(3) of this Act, to be enforced as of 23 March 2018).

273. Moreover, when the child under protection pursuant to the above provisions turns 18 years old, or when the goal of the protection is deemed achieved, the head of his/her competent local government should end the relevant protective measures or discharge the child from the welfare facility in accordance with the procedures and methods prescribed by the Presidential Decree (Article 16(1) of this Act). On the contrary, the protection period may be extended if there are certain grounds as prescribed by law (Article 16(4) of this Act, to be enforced as of 23 March 2018). Also, the head of a competent local government has a duty to conduct follow-ups, such as providing guidance and management needed to promote the welfare of the child, for the child subject to protection who has returned to his/her home upon the completion of the protective measures (Article 16(2) of this Act, to be enforced as of 23 March 2018).

II. Prevention of and Measures Against Child Abuse

274. The Child Welfare Act imposes a duty of precaution and prevention of child abuse on the State and the local governments in order to deal with the problem of child abuse (referring to harms done to a child's health or welfare or physical, mental or sexual violence, or cruel acts that are likely to impede normal growth of a child committed by adults, including the child's protector, or an act of abandoning or neglecting a child by the child's protector. *See* Article 3(7) of this Act) (Article 22 of this Act).

275. The head of an agency specializing in child protection needs to check whether any child abuse has recurred even after an act of child abuse came to an end, and may provide the necessary assistance. He/she should provide support for the abused child and his/her family members, such as counselling, education, medical treatment and psychological therapy, to ensure the child's safety and the home's sound functioning (Articles 28 and 29 of this Act).

276. Furthermore, the Act on Special Cases concerning the Punishment, etc. of Child Abuse Crimes stipulates the punishment of child abuse crimes and the procedures therefor, the procedures to protect the abused child, and the protective orders against child abusers, thereby reinforcing child protection. With regard to the punishment, the regulations on punishment have been reinforced by creating a crime of death resulting from child abuse and a crime of aggravated bodily injury on children resulting from child abuse and making them carry a sentence of up to life in prison. In addition, habitual offenders and persons working in child welfare facilities are to receive aggravated punishment (Articles 4 through 7 of the Act on Special Cases). Moreover, when a child abuser caused a child serious injuries, or when he/she has committed child abuse crimes repeatedly, a prosecutor may request the court to sentence the loss of the parental rights (Article 9 of the Act on Special Cases).

277. As for protective orders, anyone can report child abuse crimes to an agency specializing in child protection or an investigative agency, and persons working in child welfare facilities are obliged to report child abuse crimes (Article 10 of the Act on Special Cases). When such report is received, a judicial police officer or an employee of an agency specializing in child protection should go to the scene of the crime without delay (Article 11 of the Act on Special Cases). The judicial police officer or the employee who went to or discovered the scene of a child abuse crime should take certain emergency measures to protect the abused child (Article 12 of the Act on Special Cases). Apart from such emergency measures, a prosecutor may request the court to approve an ad hoc measure when he/she acknowledges a risk of the crime recurring (Article 14 of the Act on Special Cases), and a judge may approve an ad hoc measure against the child abuser when deemed necessary to facilitate the investigation and hearing of the crime or to protect the abused child (Article 19 of the Act on Special Cases). If there remains a risk of the child abuse crime recurring despite a judicial police officer's emergency measures, or if the case is so pressing that the officer cannot wait for the court's approval of an ad hoc measure, then the officer may take a limited range of measures, such as isolation of the victim from his/her residence and a denial of access, either ex officio or upon the request of an abused child, his/her legal representative excluding the child abuser, his/her attorney or the head of an agency specializing in child protection (Article 13 of the Act on Special Cases).

278. Apart from such temporary and emergency measures, the court may issue protective orders for child protection cases (Article 36 of the Act on Special Cases), or issue a protection order for the abused child (Article 47 of the Act on Special Cases). The protective orders include restrictions on a child abuse offender's access to a child victim or his/her family members, restriction on or suspension of the exercise of parental rights or guardian's authority over a child victim, community service, lecture attendance order and/or probation under the Act on Probation, etc., entrustment to facilities for care and custody established under the control of the Minister of Justice or to protective facilities designated by the Minister of Justice, entrustment to medical institutions for treatment, and entrustment to agencies specializing in child protection or counselling centres for counselling. These orders can be imposed concurrently. The protection orders include isolation of a child abuse offender from a child victim, including evacuation from the residence of a child victim or a room occupied by him/her, restriction on the access of a child abuse offender to a child victim or his/her family members, entrusting a child victim to child welfare facilities, restriction on or suspension of the exercise of parental rights over a child victim by a person with parental rights who is a child abuse offender, restriction on or suspension of the exercise of guardian's authority over a child victim by a guardian who is a child abuse offender, and decision in substitution for the expression of will by a person with parental rights or a guardian. These orders can also be imposed concurrently.

§2. Measures for Children Subject to Support

I. Support for the Child's Safety and Health

279. The State is responsible for establishing the safety standards for child welfare facilities and goods for children and having the manufacturers, installers and managers of child's goods observe them (Article 30 of this Act). The heads of child welfare facilities, daycare centres, kindergartens, and elementary and secondary schools are responsible for establishing education plans on prevention of sexual violence and child abuse, precaution and prevention of disappearance and abduction, prevention of drug abuse, safety measures against disasters, and traffic safety by taking the age of children subject to education into consideration and carrying out such education. These plans need to be reported to the competent authorities once a year (Article 31 of this Act). Moreover, if deemed necessary to protect children, the government may designate surrounding areas of urban parks, daycare centres, elementary schools, special education schools and kindergartens as child protection zones, take necessary measures, and place and utilize the manpower for the protection of the safety of the children (Articles 32 and 33 of this Act).

280. The central and local governments should provide support to promote children's health and physical strength (Article 35 of this Act), and public health centres are in charge of preventing contagious diseases among children, health counselling and physical examinations of children, guidance on their health and sanitation, and improvement of children's nutrition (Article 36 of this Act).

II. Support for Children in Vulnerable Social Groups

281. The State and local governments choose households whose conditions for the growth of children and welfare are vulnerable and provide an integrated service that offers comprehensive support for health, welfare, protection, education, and medical treatment of the child subject to support and other family members of such households, with an aim to promote the child's healthy growth and development (Article 37 of this Act). A vulnerable household means the household of a beneficiary under the Act on National Basic Living Security, the household of lowest-income earners, or the household the growth of children and welfare conditions of which are vulnerable as determined by the Minister of Health and Welfare (Article 37(1) of the Enforcement Decree of the Child Welfare Act). The integrated service covers health promotion services, such as medical check-up and education on disease prevention, support of the child's basic learning, education to develop the child's sociability and emotions, parental guidance on raising children, and other services required to promote the child's growth and development. In order to carry out the tasks for such integrated services, the Minister of Health and Welfare, a mayor, a governor, or the head of a Si/Gun/Gu (city, county, district) should establish and operate organizations supporting the integrated service that consist of public officials and civil professionals (Article 37(2) and 37(3) of the Enforcement Decree of this Act).

282. In order to support children's self-reliance after the termination of protection of children subject to protection in foster homes or the discharge from child welfare facilities, the State and local governments should take measures, such as support for the residence, living, education and employment, support for the formation and management of assets required for self-reliance ('asset formation support'), factual survey and research on self-reliance, and the establishment and operation of a follow-up management system (Articles 38 and 42 of this Act).

283. The Minister of Health and Welfare may establish the Council for Promotion of Support for Children's Self-Reliance that consists of public officials from relevant administrative agencies in order to implement the policies for supporting self-reliance of children subject to support in an efficient manner, while the central and local governments may implement asset formation support programmes to help the children become as sound members of the society (Articles 41 and 43 of this Act).

Chapter 4. Finance

284. The finance under the Child Welfare Act consists of the cost borne by the central and local governments and the payment by the welfare service users themselves.

285. The finance for child protection programmes conducted by the central and local governments is appropriated from the ordinary budget. As for the child protective measures carried out by child welfare facilities or agencies specializing in child welfare, the governments may subsidize all or part of the expenses incurred with regard to the operation of such facilities or agencies (Article 59 of this Act). The subsidy is paid for expenses incurred in establishing and operating child welfare facilities and in running their programmes, or in raising, protecting and managing the fostered children, expenses incurred in raising by proxy a child subject to protection or in protecting the child in a foster home, expenses incurred in the guidance, supervision, enlightenment and publicity of child welfare services, expenses incurred in establishing and operating agencies specializing in child welfare, expenses incurred in providing the integrated service for children in vulnerable social groups (Article 37 of this Act), expenses incurred in providing support for self-reliance of children subject to protection (Article 38 of this Act), expenses needed for the asset formation support programmes (Article 42 of this Act) and expenses needed for guiding and fostering child welfare organizations (Article 58 of this Act). However, in case the head of a programme or a facility to which the subsidy has been provided violates the conditions for the grant of the subsidy, where he/she has received the subsidy in a false or unjust manner, where he/she takes action to gain personal profits from the operation of an agency specializing in child welfare or a child welfare facility, where any remaining balance of subsidies exists, and/or where he/she violates this Act or an order issued under this Act, he/she should refund all or part of the subsidies already granted (Article 61 of this Act).

286. A mayor, a governor, the head of a Si/Gun/Gu (city, county, district), or the head of a child welfare facility is allowed to collect all or part of the expenses required for the protective measures under Article 15 of this Act (foster homes, putting the child into a child welfare facility, hospitalizing or committing a child in a specialized hospital or a care centre) or the actual expenses required for the protection and treatment of an abused child from the person him/herself or his/her obligatory provider (Article 60 of this Act; Article 55 of its Enforcement Decree). However, in the case where the person him/herself or his/her obligatory provider receives the assistance for the cost of living under other laws, the collection amount may be reduced or exempted (proviso of Article 55(1) of its Enforcement Decree).

Part XIII. Act on Welfare of Old Persons

Chapter 1. Significance and Purpose of the Act on Welfare of Old Persons

287. The Welfare of Old Persons Act (WOPA) was enacted in 1981 to seek appropriate measures to maintain physical and mental health and stable lives of the elderly, thereby contributing to the promotion of the health and welfare of older persons. Around then, the National Pension Act was yet to be enacted, and the Medical Insurance Act, which was the older version of the National Health Insurance Act, applied only to workplaces with a hundred or more full-time workers. In other words, it was before social insurance programmes began working normally as national insurance covering the entire population. The services provided under the Act on Welfare of Old Persons were also limited: they were mainly about hiring counsellors for the welfare of the elderly to provide counselling and guidance services, performing medical check-ups for the senior citizens aged 65 or older, helping senior citizens be admitted to welfare facilities for the elderly under 'user pays principle' if necessary, and providing preferential treatments for transportation or public facilities.

288. Since then, with a low birth-rate, an increase in life expectancy, and a sharp growth in the elderly population, Korea is expected to become an aged society (an aged society means a society in which the population of older persons aged 65 or older accounts for 14% or more of the total population. Korea's elderly population is estimated to reach 12.22% in 2013 and 14% in 2017) at a rapid pace. This has led to growing social awareness on the problems related to the ageing population. Accordingly, a systematic and comprehensive system for the services for the elderly in consideration of their demand for welfare is called for. Considering the physical characteristics of the elderly, three services, i.e., minimum income security, health and medical services and care services, should be provided organically. Plus, the foundation for the welfare of the elderly will be established only when the measures to actualize social participation of the elderly are secured. For this reason, the Act on Welfare of Old Persons introduced the old-age allowance system in 1991 and the old-age pension system in 1998, but they were abolished upon the enforcement of the Basic Old-Age Pension Act in 2008. Also, as the Basic Pension Act came into force in 2014, the Basic Old-Age Pension Act was abolished. Since 1989, welfare facilities for the elderly have been subdivided into several categories and diversified, which enabled demand-oriented, customized welfare services. Some functions overlap inevitably with the Act on Long-Term Care Insurance for Older

Persons (*see* Chapter 3), which was enforced in 2008. From 1998, more detailed measures started being put into practice to promote social participation and employment of the elderly.

289. The Act on Welfare of Old Persons is responsible for meeting the welfare demand apart from long-term care benefits under the Act on Long-Term Care Insurance for Older Persons and basic pension under the Basic Pension Act. Its fundamental ideas are about ensuring stable lives for the elderly, guaranteeing them opportunities to participate in social activities based on their abilities and having them contribute to social development by maintaining their health and utilizing their knowledge and experience (*see* Article 2 of this Act). However, the most important and urgent challenge is welfare measures to protect the older persons in blind spot who benefit from neither long-term care benefits nor basic pension systems. The current Act on Welfare of Old Persons stipulates that its purpose is 'to contribute to promoting the health and welfare of older persons by preventing or detecting their diseases early, maintaining their mental and physical health through proper treatment and recuperation according to their specific conditions, and taking appropriate measures to ensure stable lives of older persons' (Article 1). Therefore, this Act needs to be operated in close connection with other social security systems for the health and life stability of the elderly.

Chapter 2. Persons Subject to Protection

290. Although this Act does not expressly specify those subject to protection, it generally protects older persons aged 65 or older. Upon its revision on 2 December 2016, this Act amended Article 39-9 (Prohibited Acts) and defined in that provision that the elderly means persons aged 65 or older. This clarification was made because there had been problems in imposing punishments to those who engaged in 'prohibited acts against the elderly' when it was ambiguous who 'the elderly' was. Also, it was because the provision on obligations for reporting elder abuse for those who work in certain professions (Article 39-6(2) of this Act) did not have the age standard that defines the elderly subject to this provision. In other words, excluding these provisions, anyone under 65 may be protected under this Act as long as he/she shows significant signs of decrepitude and is acknowledged to require special protection thereunder (e.g., Article 28 of this Act).

Chapter 3. Categories and Substance of Benefits

291. This Act stipulates welfare measures to promote social participation of the elderly and support their income and livelihoods, such as support for their social participation, support for their living, and preferential treatments; medical check-ups as ordinary and preventive welfare measures; counselling services for and admission of senior citizens who require special protection to welfare facilities for the elderly; and other welfare measures such as rehabilitation and care programmes.

§1. Medical Check-Ups

292. The Minister of Health and Welfare, a mayor, a governor, or the head of a Si/Gun/Gu (city, county, district) (hereinafter referred to as a 'welfare services agency') should conduct medical check-ups for the elderly aged 65 or older in national and public hospitals, community health centres or other designated medical examination institutions at least once every two years, up to secondary check-ups depending on their physical condition (Article 27 of this Act; Article 20 of its Enforcement Decree).

§2. Counselling and Admission to Welfare Facilities

293. A welfare services agency should take the following measures when it deems necessary for the promotion of the welfare of the elderly: (i) a person aged 65 or older, or a person who protects such older person should receive counselling and guidance from relevant public officials or counsellors for the welfare of the elderly; (ii) a person aged 65 or older for whom protection at home is impracticable due to his/her physical, mental, economic or other circumstantial reasons should be admitted to residential welfare facilities for the elderly or home-care welfare facilities for the elderly; and (iii) a person aged 65 or older who needs continuous protection due to his/her serious physical or mental defects and for whom protection at home is impracticable due to his/her economic reasons should be admitted to medical welfare facilities for the elderly. These measures can be taken for a person under 65 years old if he/she shows significant signs of decrepitude and therefore requires special protection (Article 28 of this Act). On top of that, protective measures should be taken for senior citizens living alone, such as providing visiting care service and checking their safety (Article 27-2 of this Act).

§3. Rehabilitation and Care Programmes for the Elderly

294. The central and local governments may carry out rehabilitation and care programmes for older persons who need physical and mental rehabilitation and care (Article 30 of this Act). To do so, a welfare services agency may provide community health centres or welfare facilities for the elderly with professionals and equipment needed for health promotion, prevention of geriatric diseases and rehabilitation and care of the elderly. Also, it should develop and distribute rehabilitation and care programmes (Article 13 of its Enforcement Decree).

§4. Measures for Social Participation and Support for Living

295. A welfare services agency has to make efforts to expand the social participation of the elderly. Such efforts include enhancing opportunities for older persons to engage in community services, establishing policies to develop and distribute professions suitable for older persons, and providing employment opportunities to older persons who have the ability to work (Article 23(1) of this Act). As part of these efforts, a welfare services agency may: (i) provide necessary assistance to other welfare agencies for the elderly, such as community service agencies of the elderly and job placement agencies for the elderly, to promote community services and employment of the elderly (Article 23(2) of this Act); or (ii) establish and run an agency dedicated to developing and distributing jobs suitable for the ability and aptitude of older persons and providing necessary education and training for them or entrust its operations in part or in full to a corporation or an organization (Article 23-2 of this Act). Moreover, if a highly respected and experienced elderly person wishes to engage in community services, he/she may be commissioned as a community service counsellor and take charge of certain tasks (Article 24 of this Act).

296. In addition, as part of the support for the living of the elderly, when granting permission for or entrusting the installation of stores or vending machines that sell daily necessities, such as food, office supplies and newspapers, in the public facilities established and operated by the central government or local governments or other public agencies, an application made by a person aged 65 or older should be given a priority (Article 25 of this Act).

297. Moreover, preferential treatments are provided for the elderly, enabling them to use transportations operated by the central or local governments and public facilities, including palaces, royal tombs, museums and parks, for free or at discounted prices. Furthermore, the government may encourage those who operate a business related to the daily lives of the elderly to offer reduced charges to older persons aged 65 or older and may extend appropriate assistance to such business operators in those cases (Article 26 of this Act).

§5. Prohibition of Elder Abuse

298. This Act presents the fundamental ideas that the elderly should be respected for their contribution to the raising of descendants and the social development, and therefore they should be granted sound and stable lives (Article 2(1) of this Act). A provision prohibiting the elder abuse is expressly stipulated therein as one of the concrete measures to realize the fundamental ideas. Elder abuse means an act of physical, mental, emotional and sexual violence, and economic exploitation of, or atrocities against, or desertion or neglect of an elder person (Article 1-2(4) of this

Act). More specifically, the following acts are prohibited: (i) an act of violence against an elderly person, or an act inflicting an injury thereon; (ii) an act of sexual violence or harassment that gives a sense of sexual shame to an elderly person; (iii) an act of desertion of an elderly person under one's own protection or supervision, or an act of neglecting basic needs, including food, clothing and shelter, as well as medical treatment thereof; (iv) an act of making an elder person beg, or an act of begging for something by utilizing an elderly person; (v) an act of using the money and valuables donated or provided for an elderly person for purposes other than their original purpose; and (vi) an act of emotional abuse harming the mental health of an elderly person, such as verbal abuse, threats and menace (Article 39-9 of this Act). Anyone who gets to know about any of the above abusive acts may file a report to an institution specializing in the protection of the elderly or an investigation agency. In particular, a healthcare provider who practices medicine, the head and a staff member of welfare facilities for the elderly, a person providing counselling, medical treatment, training or care services for the elderly with disabilities in welfare facilities, a counsellor at a domestic violence counselling centre, a staff member of a shelter for victims of domestic violence, a counsellor for the welfare of the elderly at welfare facilities for the elderly, and a public official dedicated to social welfare are obliged to report the case to an institution specializing in the protection of the elderly or an investigation agency when he/she comes to know about the elder abuse while performing his/her duties (Article 39-6 of this Act).

§6. Welfare Facilities for the Elderly

299. This Act enumerates residential welfare facilities for the elderly, medical welfare facilities for the elderly, leisure welfare facilities for the elderly, home-care welfare facilities for the elderly and institutions specializing in the protection of the elderly as welfare facilities for the elderly (Article 31 of this Act). To ensure adequate management, the methods and substance of the regulations imposed on the facilities are different according to their type and the principal agents of their programmes.

300. First, residential welfare facilities for the elderly include an institution for older persons, which intends to provide those admitted with meals and other conveniences necessary for their daily lives; a communal living home for the elderly, which intends to provide them with home-like residential environments, meals and other conveniences necessary for their daily lives; and a welfare house for the elderly, which intends to provide conveniences necessary for their daily lives, such as convenient residence, guidance and counselling, and safety management, through a lease of housing facility to the elderly (Article 32). A person aged 60 or older is qualified to be admitted to a welfare house for the elderly, and his/her spouse is allowed to be admitted together even if he/she is under 60 years old (Article 33-2). Second, medical welfare facilities for the elderly include a care facility for the elderly, which provides meals, medical treatment and other convenience necessary for the daily lives of those senior persons who need assistance because of their geriatric diseases, such as dementia and paralysis, and medical treatment and communal living centre for the elderly, which provides a home-like residential environment, meals, medical treatment and other convenience necessary for the daily lives of the senior persons described above (Article 34). Third, leisure welfare facilities for the elderly include a welfare centre for the elderly, a senior citizens' centre, educational classes for the elderly, which encourage activities related to their interests and hobbies and promote their social participation (Article 36), and last but not least, home-care welfare facilities for the elderly provide visiting care service, day and night protection services, short-term protection services and visiting bath services (Article 38).

301. The above welfare facilities for the elderly may be established by the central or local governments (Articles 33(1), 35(1), 37(1) and 39(1) of this Act), or by any qualified person after registering with the head of Si/Gun/Gu (city, county, district) (Articles 33(2), 33(3), 35(2), 35(3), 37(2), 37(4), 39(2) and 39(3) of this Act). For the registration of the establishment, such a facility should meet the requirements on the facility, manpower and operation as prescribed by the Minister of Health and Welfare. However, as for medical welfare facilities for the elderly, the matters necessary for both the registration of the establishment and the permission to the establishment should be prescribed separately (*see* Article 35(3) of this Act).

Chapter 4. Basic Pension System

§1. Significance

302. In the past, the Act on Welfare of Old Persons would provide old-age pension to the elderly. However, there was a dispute over insufficient criteria for selection of the beneficiaries and level of benefits, and it was replaced by the Basic Old-Age Pension Act, which was enforced on 1 January 2008. Then, on 20 May 2014, the Basic Pension Act was established to secure fiscal sustainability, create a stable public pension system for the elderly generation and provide basic pension to 70% of the elderly aged 65 or older who have weak income base, thereby addressing the poverty issue of the elderly and contributing to their stable livelihood and welfare. The Basic Pension Act came into effect as of 1 July 2014.

§2. Persons Subject to Protection

303. A person eligible for basic pension is a person aged 65 or older, whose 'assessed income', i.e., the sum of the assessed amount of income and the income-equivalent of their property, is lower than the amount determined and publicly announced by the Minister of Health and Welfare (As of 2020, the minimum amount for selection is KRW 1.48 million for a single household and KRW 2.368 million for a couple household). When determining the minimum amount for selection, it is ensured that the number of beneficiaries of basic pensions accounts for 70% of the total number of persons aged 65 or older (Article 3 of the Basic Pension Act).

§3. Application for and Decision on Basic Pension

304. A person who wishes to receive a basic pension or his/her representative prescribed by the Ordinance of the Ministry of Health and Welfare may file an application for the payment of basic pension with the mayor of a special self-governing city, the governor of a special self-governing province, or the head of a Si/Gun/Gu (city, county, district) (Article 10 of the Basic Pension Act). Upon the application, an investigation is conducted, and the eligibility for basic pension is determined (Article 13). In order to prevent an older person from missing his/her opportunity to be entitled to a basic pension for unjust reasons, such as lack of information, the Minister of Health and Welfare or the head of the local government should provide persons aged 65 or older with the information related to the basic pension, such as eligibility, pension amount and application method (Article 10-2). Moreover, to protect the beneficiary's rights and ensure a reasonable investigation, the Minister of Health and Welfare, the mayor of a special self-governing city, the governor of a special self-governing province, or the head of a Si/Gun/Gu (city, county, district) may have public officials under his/her control to visit the residence or other necessary places of the qualified recipients of basic pension and investigate documents or ask necessary questions to related persons (Article 11(1)). The official who pays a visit, conducts an investigation and asks questions should carry a document indicating his/her authority, investigation period, the scope of investigation, the person in charge of the investigation, relevant statutes, etc. and show it to the related persons (Article 11(3)).

§4. Calculation of the Amount of Basic Pension Benefits

305. The 'standard pension benefits' shall be publicly notified each year by the Minister of Health and Welfare, based on the Fluctuation Rate of Nationwide Consumer Price Index. As of 2019, the amount is KRW 253,750. According to the amendments made in January 2021 (to come into effect in 2021), the basic pension benefits applied to the persons aged 65 or older, whose assessed income does not exceed 40/100, shall be KRW 300,000. As for the insured of the national pension plan, the basic pension amount is adjusted by reducing an amount calculated based on an amount of benefits reflecting income redistribution (two thirds) among the national pension benefits to which he/she is entitled from the standard pension benefits. As for an uninsured of the national pension plan, a person to whom the payment of the national pension has been suspended, a beneficiary of pensions for persons with disabilities and a recipient under the national basic living security system, standard pension benefits are paid as basic pension (Article 5 of the Basic Pension Act and Article 6 of the supplementary provision).

306. Basic pension goes through the evaluation of its adequacy and the adjustment in consideration of national finance. The Minister of Health and Welfare evaluates the appropriateness of basic pension amount by taking into consideration the living standards of eligible recipients of basic pension and the national consumer price inflation rate every five years, studies the actual condition of the poverty of senior citizens, makes a prospect of long-term financial requirements, and adjust standard pension benefits reflecting the result of the adequacy evaluation (Article 9).

§5. Follow-Up on Basic Pension Beneficiaries

307. If a recipient of basic pension is confined in a correctional institution or a medical treatment and detention facility or stays overseas for at least sixty consecutive days, the payment of basic pension to him/her will be suspended. In addition, if a recipient of a basic pension dies or loses his/her nationality, his/her entitlement to basic pension will be lost (Article 16). The recipient should report it with the authorities when the reason for the suspension of the payment of basic pension disappears later on, when a reason for the loss of the entitlement arises, or when any change occurs in his/her income or property (Article 18(1)). In case a person bound in duty to give the notification under the Act on the Registration, Etc. of Family Relationships has reported the death of the recipient of basic pension thereunder, such report is considered as the report of the loss of the entitlement under the Act on Welfare of Old Persons to improve the convenience of the public and raise the administrative efficiency (Article 18(2)).

308. When the basic pension is wrongfully paid, the paid basic pension amount should be collected. When a basic pension is received by fraudulent or other wrongful means, the interest should be collected in addition to the paid basic pension amount (Article 19).

§6. FINANCE

309. Under the Basic Pension Act, the basic old-age pension is financed by the state and local governments. The State shall apportion the expense prescribed by Presidential Decree in the range from 40% to 90% of the expenses incurred in relation to the payment of a basic pension, taking into consideration the demographic ratio of senior citizens, financial condition, etc. of local governments (Article 25(1), details of the ratio can be found in the Presidential Decree Article 23(1)). Any remainder after deducting the expense to be borne by the State under paragraph (1) shall be mutually shared among the Special Metropolitan City, a Metropolitan City, a Special Self-Governing City, a Special Self-Governing Province (hereinafter referred to as 'City/Do') and a Si/Gun/Gu (referring to an autonomous Gu). In this regard, the burden rate thereof shall be prescribed by municipal ordinance of each City/Do and Si/Gun/Gu, following consultations with the Minister of Health and Welfare, taking into consideration the demographic ratio of senior citizens and financial condition, etc. (Article 25(2)).

Selected Bibliography

Kwang-Seok Cheon, Ji-Soon Park & Bok-Gi Kim, Social Security Law, 6th edition, Seoul, 2020 (전광석, 박지순, 김복기, 사회보장법, 6 판, 서울, 2020).

Kwang-Seok Cheon, Korean Social Security Law, 12th edition, Seoul, 2019 (전광석, 한국사회보장법론, 12 판, 서울, 2019).

Sang-Yoon Lee, Social Security Law, Paju, 2012 (이상윤, 사회보장법, 파주, 2012).

Elim Kim, Social Security Law, Seoul, 2020 (김엘림,사회보장법, 서울, 2020).

Selected Bibliography

Index

The numbers here refer to paragraph numbers.

Index

www.ingramcontent.com/pod-product-compliance
Ingram Content Group UK Ltd.
Pitfield, Milton Keynes, MK11 3LW, UK
UKHW020147290926
15471UKWH00004B/748